Mensa
The High IQ Society

THE ALL-NEW PUZZLE BOOK

D1337374

THIS IS A CARLTON BOOK

Published in 2016 by
Carlton Books
20 Mortimer Street
London W1T 3JW

ISBN: 978-1-78097-514-6

All images: © iStockphoto & Shutterstock

Printed in Dubai

Mensa
The High IQ Society

THE ALL-NEW
PUZZLE
BOOK

MORE THAN 200 ENIGMAS,
PUZZLES AND CONUNDRUMS

Tim Dedopulos

CARLTON
BOOKS

Mensa is the international society for people with a high IQ.
We have more than 100,000 members in over 40 countries worldwide.

The society's aims are:
   to identify and foster human intelligence for the benefit of humanity
   to encourage research in the nature, characteristics, and uses of intelligence
   to provide a stimulating intellectual and social environment for its members

Anyone with an IQ score in the top two per cent of population is eligible to become a member of Mensa – are you the 'one in 50' we've been looking for?

Mensa membership offers an excellent range of benefits:
   Networking and social activities nationally and around the world
   Special Interest Groups – hundreds of chances to pursue your hobbies and interests – from art to zoology!
   Monthly members' magazine and regional newsletters
   Local meetings – from games challenges to food and drink
   National and international weekend gatherings and conferences
   Intellectually stimulating lectures and seminars
   Access to the worldwide SIGHT network for travellers and hosts

For more information about Mensa: www.mensa.org, or

British Mensa Ltd.,
St John's House,
St John's Square,
Wolverhampton
WV2 4AH
Telephone: +44 (0) 1902 772771
E-mail: services@mensa.org.uk
www.mensa.org.uk

Contents

INTRODUCTION

INTRODUCTION

Welcome to this book, which contains 200 puzzles of every conceivable variety. They will test your little grey cells, and should make even the most hardened of puzzlers scratch your heads in frustration.

The questions in the expert-compiled book will pose a wide range of problems, some of them highly complex. They're designed to challenge your faculties in areas including logical reasoning, deductive inference, spatial awareness, mathematics, word patterns, and more. You'll be poring over the contents for quite some time. If you find that you need to head to the back of the book to discover an answer, don't feel bad – everyone has different areas of strength. Besides, you'll have given your brain a good workout, and that's what counts the most.

Broadly speaking, the puzzles in this book usually fall into one (or more!) of five separate categories.

1. Logical Reasoning is the backbone of any puzzle collection. You are given a set of information, and from that information, you are required to think your way through the steps required to arrive at the answer. The purest tests of logical reasoning require absolutely no prior knowledge, but logical thinking is such an integral part of puzzling that it crops up in the vast majority of questions.

2. Lateral Thinking challenges your mental flexibility. Sometimes, you need

to deviate from the apparent path. None of the puzzles in this book are arbitrary or unfair, but some of them may not be quite what they seem to be at first glance. So if you just can't seem to come to an answer, perhaps it's time to set aside your assumptions, and take a step sideways into the thorny territory of "what else could this represent?"

3. Spatial Awareness is a vitally important aspect of intelligence. One of the strongest correlates of a good IQ is the ability to take abstract visual information and manipulate it as if it were part of objective reality. Working with data in this way allows for new lines of deduction and inference to be drawn, increasing the information you have to work with.

4. Word Patterns explore your facility both with written language, and with symbolism, which is at the root of all writing. Another strong correlate with intelligence, facility with language is the prime requisite for communication – and without communication, there can be no sharing of ideas or new knowledge.

5. Mathematical and Informational problems seek to test your knowledge as well as your puzzle-solving ability. Intelligence is at its strongest when it is applied from a firm grounding in real data. Genius is uncovered in action, not in potential. So these puzzles will test your awareness of maths and other facts as well as your problem-solving skills.

The importance of these facilities is probably why we, humanity, have been using puzzles to test our mental prowess since the very earliest days of our species. Puzzles are ubiquitous; there is no culture, current or historic, that we have good information from which has not been found to include puzzles. Even the very earliest examples of writing include clear evidence of them.

Our desire to solve mental challenges is hot-wired into us instinctively. It's a central component of who we are. Our brain's ability to look at the world, challenge it and manipulate it until it makes sense is one of our strongest assets. Like physical exercise, mental exercise is pleasurable on a deep, chemical level, as well as beneficial. We love to assess ourselves, we love to succeed at challenges, and we love to grow. The fact that mental exercise – solving puzzles – has now been proven to help stave off mental decline, even Alzheimer's disease, is just a happy benefit.

Although there's no strict order, you may well find that the puzzles nearer the start of the book are more straightforward than those later on. Let's be clear – solving these puzzles won't be easy. But it will be fun.

Happy puzzling.

THE PUZZLES

01

If Andrew likes the riverbank but not the shore, Michael likes the hills but not the valleys, and Malcolm likes the countryside but not the forest, which location does Thomas like?

A. The plains

B. The meadow

C. The taiga

D. The badlands

E. The tundra

Answer see page 134

Answer see page 134

02

Each symbol in the grid has a consistent value. What number should replace the question mark?

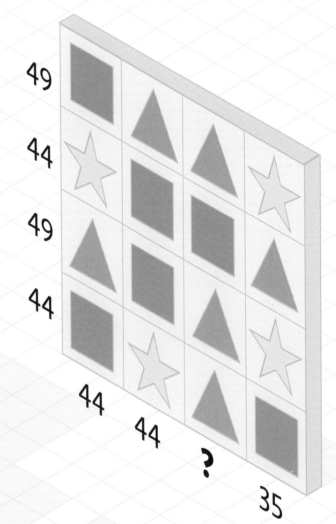

49

44

49

44

44

44

?

35

10

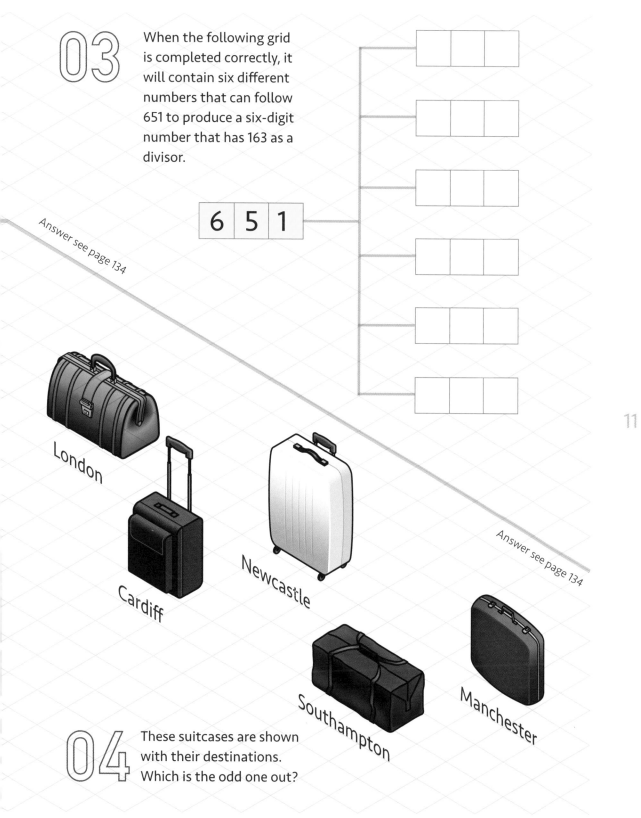

03 When the following grid is completed correctly, it will contain six different numbers that can follow 651 to produce a six-digit number that has 163 as a divisor.

| 6 | 5 | 1 |

Answer see page 134

London

Cardiff

Newcastle

Southampton

Manchester

Answer see page 134

11

04 These suitcases are shown with their destinations. Which is the odd one out?

05

Several famous musical albums have been encoded using the key below. Can you decipher them?

1	2	3	4	5	6	7	8	9
a	b	c	d	e	f	g	h	i
j	k	l	m	n	o	p	q	r
s	t	u	v	w	x	y	z	

2	5	5	9	7	5	5	1	9	1	1	2	3	9	4	1	7	9	5	9	7	8	2	9	6	5	4	5	9							
5	8	9	2	5	5	7	9	8	6	3	1	2	6	5	9	2	8	5	9	2	6	4	7	7	3	1	9	4							
7	9	5	2	9	6	3	6	7	4	9	2	8	5	9	4	1	9	2	9	1	9	4	5	9	6	6	9	2	8	5	9	4	6	6	5
3	5	3	9	5	5	9	4	9	6	5	9	6	1	3	3	9	5	7	9	9	5	2	6	9	7	6	3								

Answer see page 134

Answer see page 134

06

A group of one hundred people is made up of individuals who are either corrupt or honest. At least one of them is honest, but from any pair, at least one is corrupt.

How many of each are there?

Can you find the square which contains the number in this grid that is 3 squares from itself plus fifteen, 2 squares from itself minus twelve, 6 squares from itself plus five, and 7 squares from itself minus four? All distances are in straight orthogonal lines.

	A	B	C	D	E	F	G	H	I
1	52	9	35	11	18	16	80	7	21
2	29	15	70	89	75	9	78	86	4
3	58	26	4	6	70	52	15	72	84
4	17	37	85	54	53	87	38	97	8
5	72	21	92	83	38	2	39	56	84
6	43	61	25	96	33	19	48	39	56
7	54	62	4	47	53	17	49	31	61
8	31	94	29	7	46	11	4	75	88
9	46	8	74	96	83	51	65	36	5

13

Answer see page 134

The following tiles have been taken from a five by five square of numbers. When they have been reassembled accurately, the square will show the same five numbers reading both across and down.

Can you rebuild it?

14

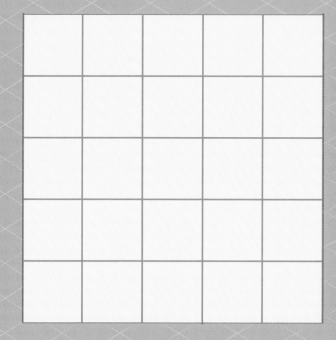

2	1	9

6	8	3

6	4	8

5	1
6	9

8	0	1
3	1	7

5	5	8	2

5	2

Answer see page 134

09 One of the squares in the 3x3 grid is incorrect. Which one?

Answer see page 134

10 Following the logic of this diagram, what symbols should the triangle at the top contain?

Answer see page 134

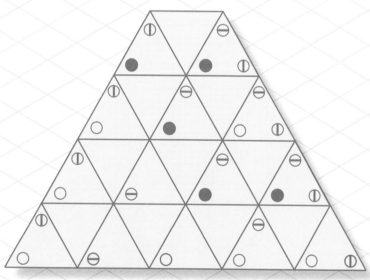

11 The following list of numbers represents places whose letters have been encoded into the numbers needed to reproduce them on a typical phone numberpad. Can you decode them?

Answer see page 134

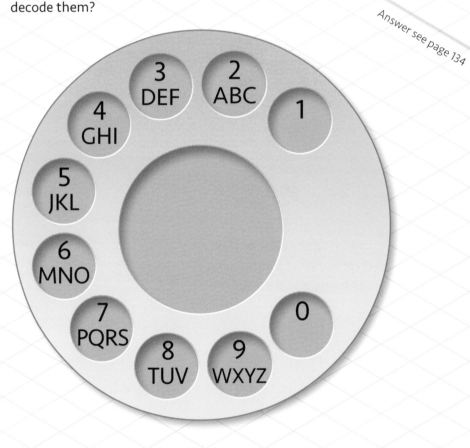

842 632

287 872 542

293 247 378 254 2

639 426

726 852 63

12 The following diagram obeys a specific logic. What should replace the question mark?

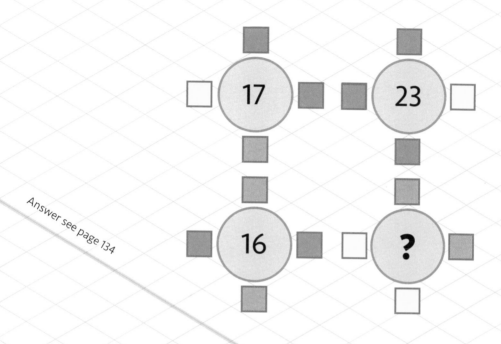

Answer see page 134

13 Using only numbers available in the grid, multiply the smallest triangular number by the largest prime number. What is the result?

Answer see page 134

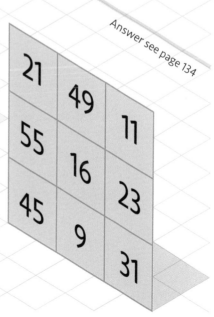

14 There is something wrong with this list. Can you tell what it is?

Bolton   Frankfurt   Portland
London   Cape Town   Athens
Chiang Mai   Rome   Muscat
Paris   Sydney   Prague
Derry   Madrid

Answer see page 134

15 The following terms are all anagrams of chemical elements. Can you disentangle them?

Answer see page 134

AIM SPOUTS

NAG ME SANE

NOBLE DUMMY

HUSH PRO OPS

NERDY HOG

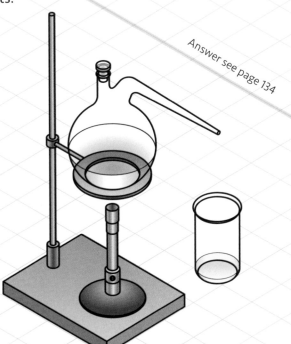

16 Taking a letter from each ball in turn, can you spell out three different world cities?

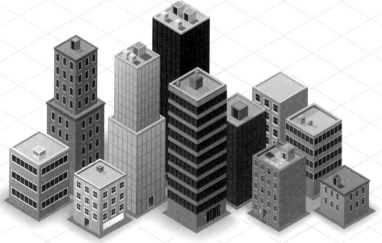

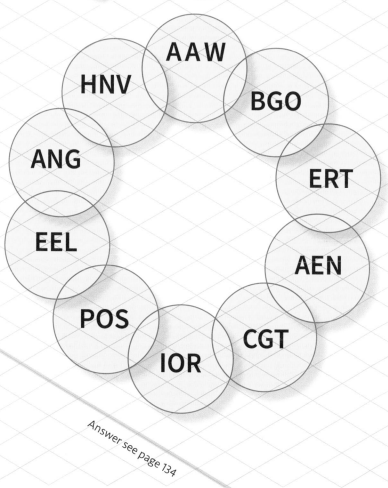

AAW

HNV

BGO

ANG

ERT

EEL

AEN

POS

CGT

IOR

Answer see page 134

Grid values:

2R 3D 2D 2L 1D
1R 3D 2L 1D 1L
2D 3R F   3L 2U
3U 1R 1D 3U 4L
3R 2U 2R 1U 1U

17 Each square on this grid shows you the move you must make to arrive at the next square in the sequence, Left, Right, Up, and/or Down. So 3R would be three squares right, and 4UL would be 4 squares diagonally up and left. Your goal is to end up on the finish square, F, having visited every square exactly once. Can you find the starting square?

Answer see page 134

18 What is the missing letter?

Answer see page 134

19 Can you arrange the following twelve words into four thematically linked groups of three?

Answer see page 134

SNOOK

PALAIC

BARBEL

GUISARME

UGARITIC

AMARANTHINE

ABLAITE

SANGUINEOUS

CHAKRAM

RASBORA

CELADON

FLAMBERGE

This grid obeys a specific sequence. However, some numbers are out of order. When shaded in, these will reveal another number. What is it?

Answer see page 134

1	5	3	7	2	6	4	8	0
9	1	7	2	6	4	8	4	8
0	7	1	5	3	7	2	8	4
8	1	9	1	5	3	7	4	6
4	9	0	9	1	5	3	6	2
6	4	8	0	9	1	5	2	7
2	6	4	8	0	9	6	5	3
7	2	6	4	8	4	9	1	5
3	7	2	6	8	8	0	9	1
5	3	7	4	6	4	8	0	9
1	5	0	7	2	6	4	8	0
9	3	5	3	7	2	6	4	8
0	5	1	5	3	7	2	6	4
8	1	9	1	5	3	7	2	6
4	9	0	9	1	5	3	7	2
6	4	9	1	5	3	7	3	7
2	6	4	8	0	9	1	5	3

21

What is K worth?

$$M + N + N = 39$$
$$K + K + L = 37$$
$$L + M + N = 41$$
$$K + L + N = 36$$

Answer see page 134

Answer see page 135

22

The following design works according to a certain logic. What number should replace the question mark?

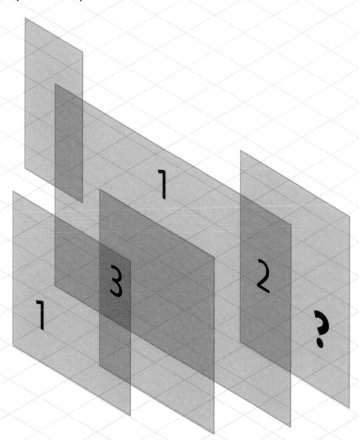

23

What is the missing letter?

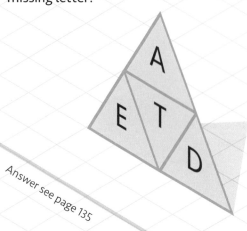

Answer see page 135

24

The following five items are all districts of a famous city. Can you decrypt them?

Answer see page 135

CQDXQJJQDJXU   GKUUDI

RHEDN   IJQJUD

RHEEABOD   YIBQDT

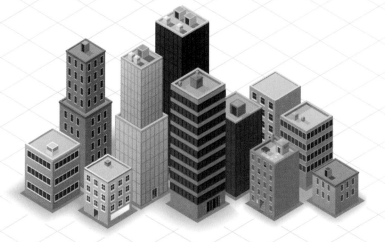

25 Can you fill in the numbers provided to correctly complete the grid?

3 digit numbers	5 digit numbers	6 digit numbers	7 digit numbers	9 digit numbers
350	12325	107613	1860589	184399096
637	50435	644059	2818249	327531981
900	57157	744858	3258302	609636074
911	58147	909137	3422047	636969961
	62658		4157622	
	82682		5636795	
	87135		7096359	
	90608		9090680	

Answer see page 135

Can you find your way
through this maze?

Answer see page 135

START

FINISH

27

Ten people are collecting their coats after a party, but it is dark, and there is some confusion. Some people may have collected the wrong coat. If nine of the people have the right coat, what is the probability that the tenth has the wrong coat?

Answer see page 135

Answer see page 135

28

Four 4-letter dog breeds jumbled are in this square. Which pair of letters is not used?

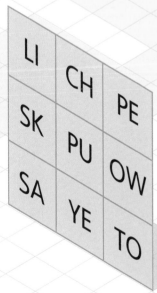

LI	CH	PE
SK	PU	OW
SA	YE	TO

29

The letters and numbers in this square obey a certain logic. What number should replace the question mark?

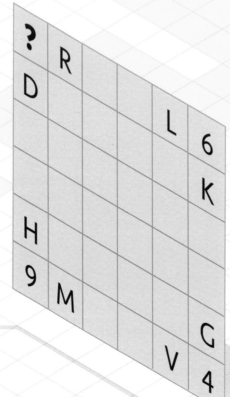

Answer see page 135

30

What single letter is missing from each grid?

Answer see page 135

C
W   C
    O   S
    ?

    G
C   A   I
    ?

A   M
    T   S
    ?

    I
B   K   N
    ?

31 This design follows a specific logic. What should replace the question mark

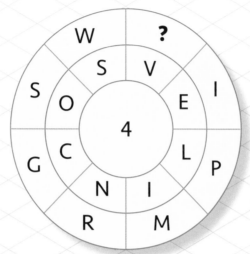

W ?
S V
S
O E I
4
G C L P
N I
R M

Answer see page 135

Answer see page 135

32 Delete all instances of letters that appear more than once, and rearrange the remainder to find the name of a city. What is it?

29

R	B	K	W	G	Q	V	J
C	N	Q	L	S	D	U	W
D	O	U	I	X	Y	P	G
Z	F	B	Z	L	A	I	D
X	Q	N	F	Q	J	T	C
T	H	V	M	P	E	O	Y

33 Two moons are orbiting a planet. One takes 30 days to make a full circuit. The other takes 5 days. If they are now in a perfect conjunction, with the quicker moon directly in between the planet and the slower moon, when will the three celestial bodies next be in the same orientation?

Answer see page 135

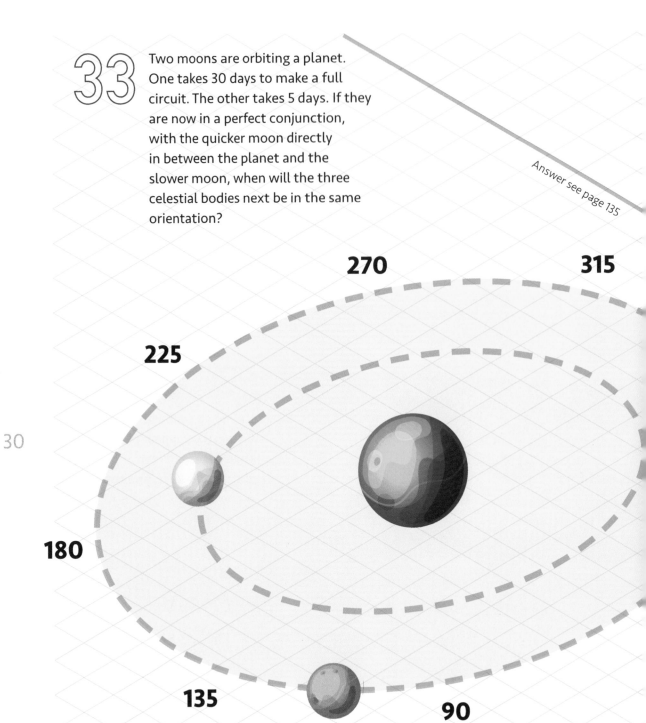

270

315

225

180

135

90

34

In the magic square below, every row, column and five-figure diagonal adds to 121. The blank spaces below each need to be filled by one of four numbers. Can you complete the square?

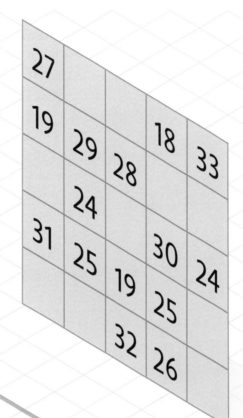

Answer see page 135

0

Answer see page 135

35

Which of these is the odd one out?

A: FORT SUMTER

B: ALAMO

C: FREDRICKSBURGH

D: CEDAR CREEK

E: SHILOH

F: FIVE FORKS

G: GETTYSBURGH

36

Which of the following numbers is not a numerical anagram of 804,331,088,950,120,324,614?

a. 580,468,043,103,819,201,342

b. 469,018,085,280,303,244,113

c. 400,800,832,192,461,543,831

d. 905,446,102,100,821,833,438

e. 960,330,324,484,180,215,810

f. 433,201,501,314,492,608,880

g. 280,135,248,018,601,039,345

h. 139,541,012,808,624,003,843

i. 280,003,314,468,410,893,152

Answer see page 135

Answer see page 135

37

There is a similarity between the two circles. Knowing that, what number should replace the question mark?

38

Which of the five options A-E below most closely matches the conditions of figure 1?

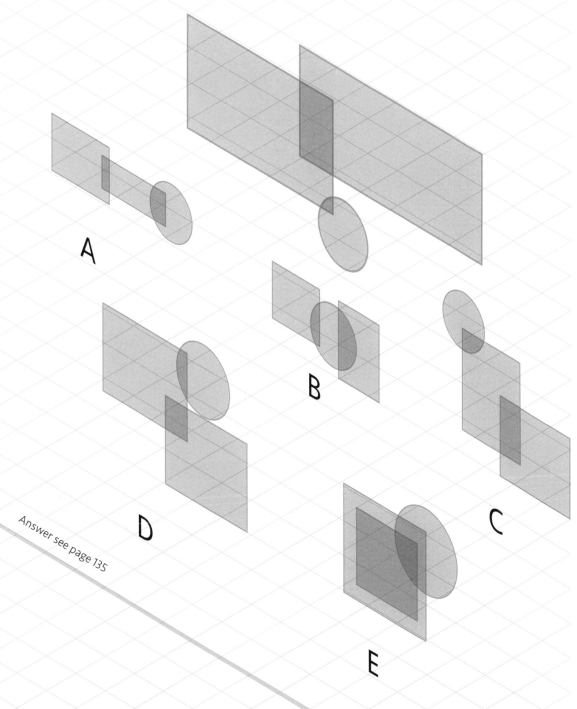

A

B

33

D

Answer see page 135

E

C

39 Which of these letters does not belong in this triangle?

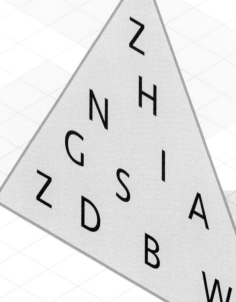

Answer see page 135

34

40 What should replace the question mark in the final square?

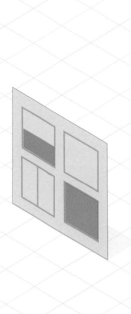

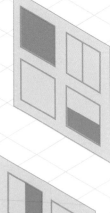

Answer see page 136

41

The following grid operates according to a specific pattern. Can you fill in the blank section?

Answer see page 136

42 Which is the odd one out?

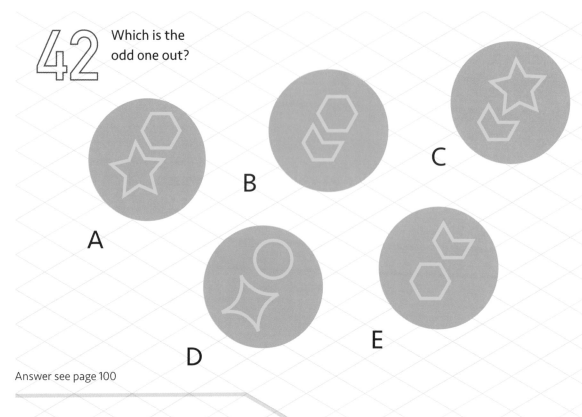

A

B

C

D

E

Answer see page 100

36

43 Find a four-digit number which divides a whole number of times into each of the numbers on the left.

6924

19619

271190

13848

3462

24234

Answer see page 100

44

Can you find the 36 numbers shown below within the number grid?

1	5	1	2	3	1	2	0	4	5	7	3	7	9	5
9	5	2	4	0	9	9	0	6	9	7	0	2	2	7
1	7	1	2	8	0	2	2	2	4	2	7	1	3	3
9	7	8	5	0	4	5	3	0	4	4	6	7	4	9
4	6	0	0	8	9	9	5	5	5	7	6	3	1	8
8	6	6	7	6	2	6	1	6	1	6	5	2	5	8
5	1	9	8	3	8	1	5	5	8	3	5	1	5	4
3	3	8	0	4	2	1	7	4	4	8	1	1	4	2
5	3	0	9	7	5	5	3	0	7	7	5	0	3	8
3	5	5	0	2	5	5	0	0	8	4	0	9	0	1
1	9	5	1	6	8	5	7	1	3	9	7	3	8	5
1	4	5	9	6	5	3	0	4	7	5	3	0	9	0
6	7	4	3	2	4	4	4	1	1	4	3	7	1	3
2	3	1	8	6	2	2	4	0	1	7	2	7	6	7
3	1	1	9	7	1	6	9	8	5	1	6	7	2	8

256	16728	280222	37495331
433	26113	975530	40172767
676	28150	980345	55508960
1758	45362	1143713	94764403
3349	63874	3186224	99069702
4423	68201	3574035	119716985
5577	110930	5184783	191948535
8379	148491	5576318	204573795
8495	158217	8005520	275125156

Answer see page 100

45 These dominos obey a certain logic. What should replace the question mark?

$\dfrac{R}{U}$

$\dfrac{K}{L}$

$\dfrac{B}{D}$

$\dfrac{D}{?}$

Answer see page 136

38

Answer see page 136

46 How many rectangles are there in this design in total?

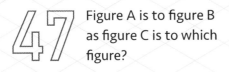

Figure A is to figure B as figure C is to which figure?

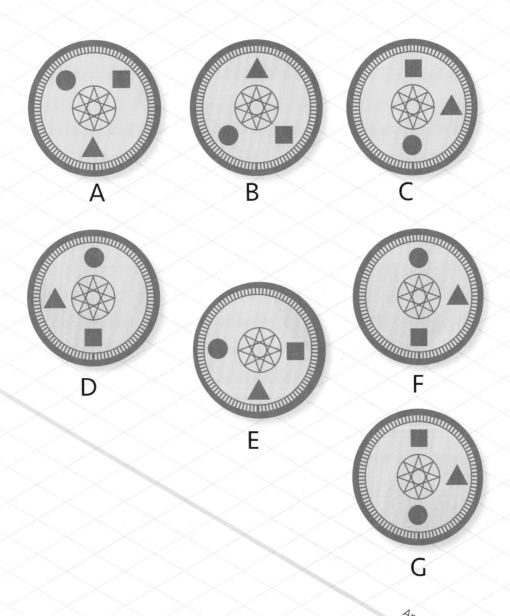

A

B

C

D

E

F

G

Answer see page 136

48 Which of the shapes below, A-D, fits with the shape above to form a perfect dark circle?

A

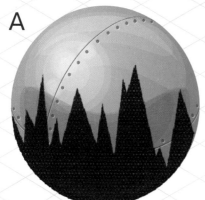

B

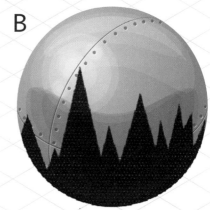

40

C

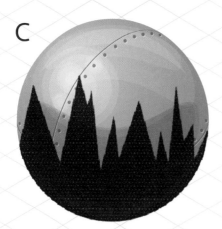

D

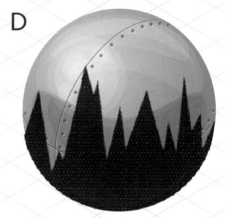

Answer see page 136

These numbers, when placed correctly into the grid, will give you two numbers which are multiples of the number 34762. Can you disentangle them?

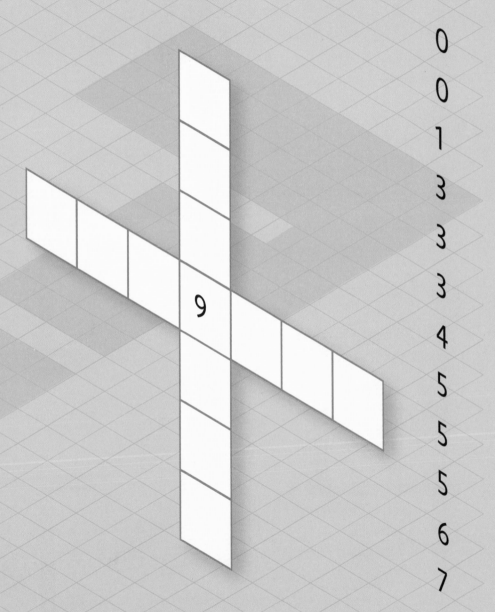

0
0
1
3
3
3
4
5
5
5
6
7

Answer see page 136

50 What are the following nouns all types of?

CRANNOG
GLACIS
CATHAIR
ABATIS
RATH

Answer see page 136

51 Examine the following sets of scales, which are in perfect balance. How many triangles are needed to balance the final scale?

Answer see page 136

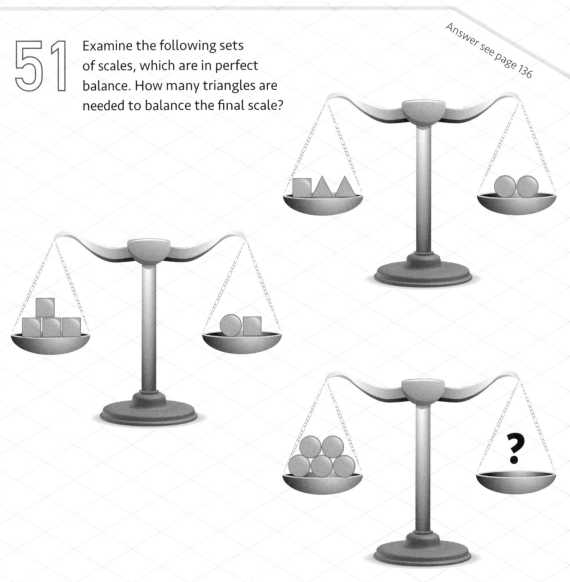

52

Which of the following is not an anagram of a current or former currency?

IRON HIDE   OAK RUN

HARD CAM   PINGS HIP

DIG RULE   ROT MASK

Answer see page 136

Answer see page 136

53

Signs – symbols in a specific position – which appear in the outer circles are transferred to the inner circle as follows: If it appears once or thrice, it is definitely transferred. If it appears twice, it is transferred if no other symbol will be transferred. If it appears four times, it is not transferred.

What does the inner circle look like?

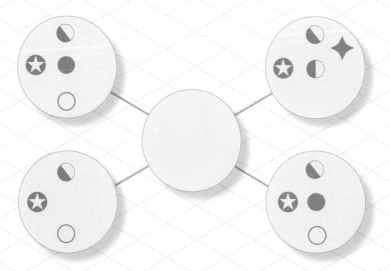

54 What weight will balance the beam?

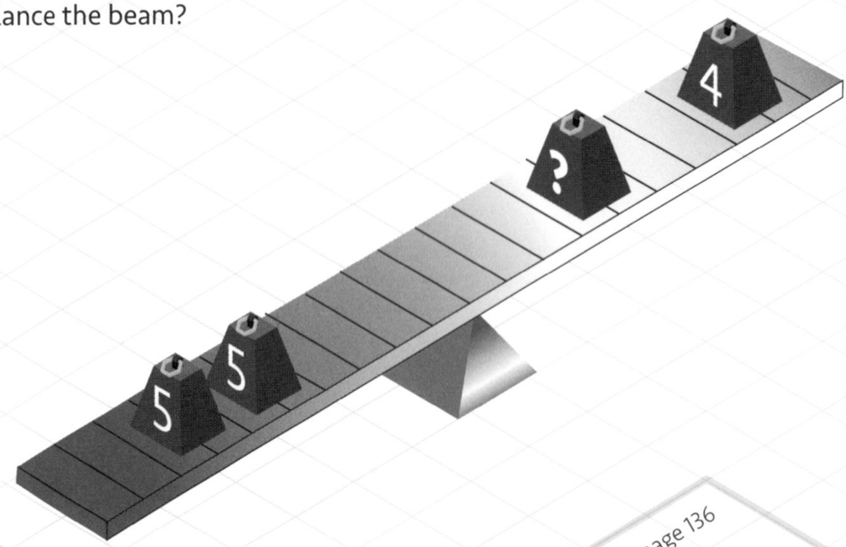

Answer see page 136

Answer see page 136

44

55 Which of these cubes cannot be made from the matrix provided?

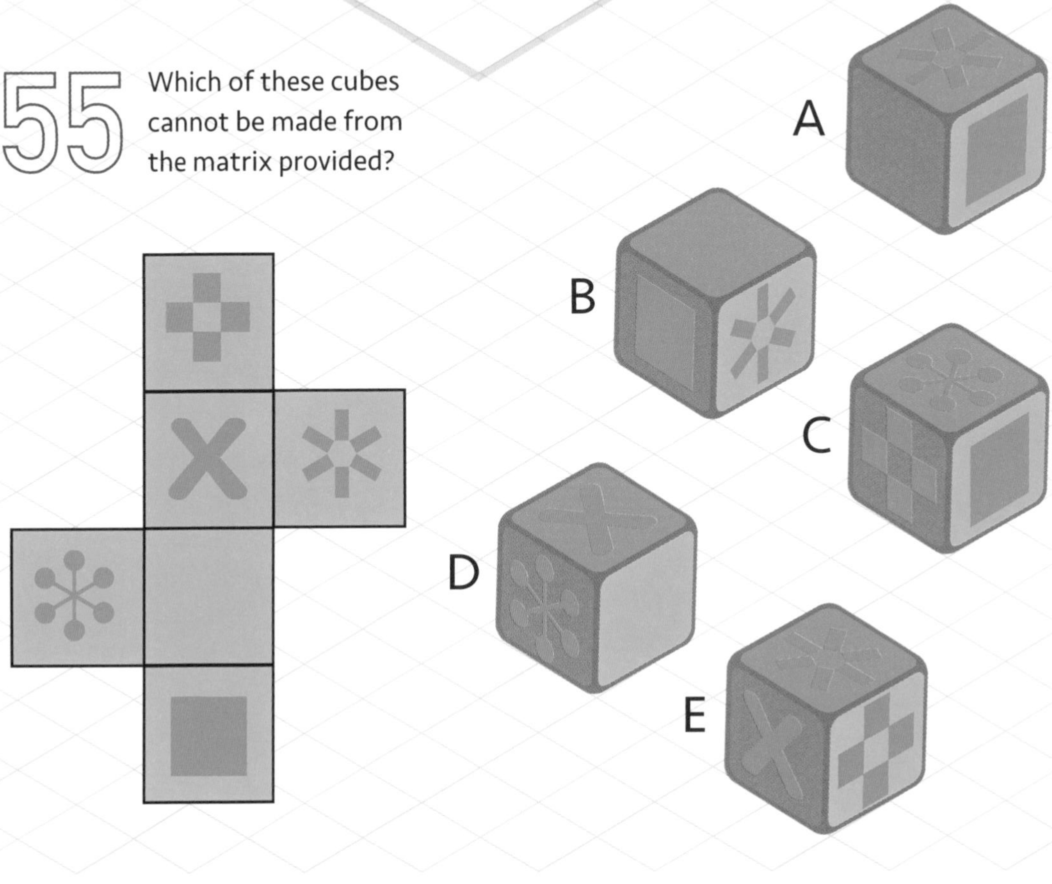

A

B

C

D

E

The numbers in this list are sequential terms in a specific sequence of numbers, but they are out of order. What is the sequence?

1 2 2 0 7 0 3 1 2 5
1 5 2 5 8 7 8 9 0 6 2 5
1 9 5 3 1 2 5
2 4 4 1 4 0 6 2 5
3 0 5 1 7 5 7 8 1 2 5
3 9 0 6 2 5
4 8 8 2 8 1 2 5
6 1 0 3 5 1 5 6 2 5
7 6 2 9 3 9 4 5 3 1 2 5
9 7 6 5 6 2 5

Answer see page 136

45

Find a three-digit number which divides a whole number of times into each of the numbers on the left.

Answer see page 136

35767

3044

362236

14459

6849

120238

58 These rings obey a certain logic. What number should replace the question mark?

Answer see page 136

Answer see page 137

59 A committee of seven needs to be drawn from twelve people. How many different ways of doing this are there?

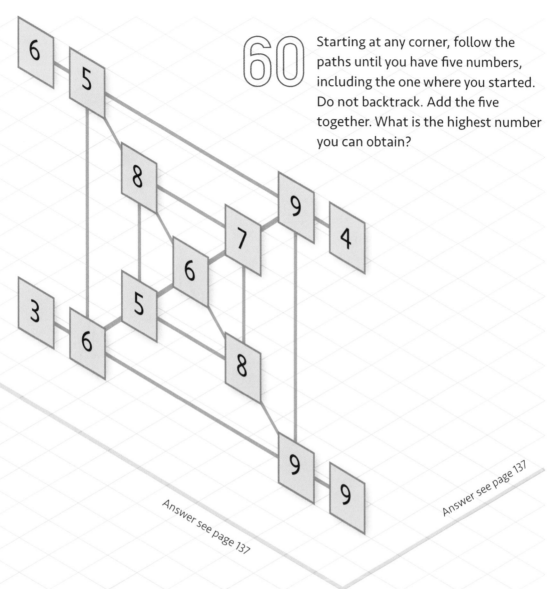

60 Starting at any corner, follow the paths until you have five numbers, including the one where you started. Do not backtrack. Add the five together. What is the highest number you can obtain?

Answer see page 137

Answer see page 137

61 Which letter is four to the right of the letter immediately to the left of the letter four to the left of the letter two to the right of the letter G?

(A) (B) (C) (D) (E) (F) (G) (H) (I) (J) (K) (L)

62 What would the next matchstick person in this sequence look like?

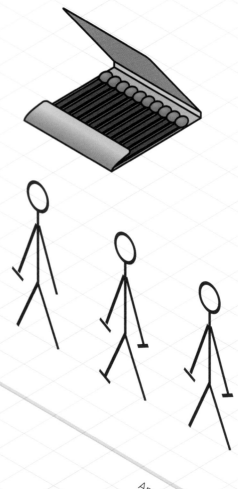

Answer see page 137

63 These pairs of circles obey a certain logic. What letter should replace the question mark?

Answer see page 137

B K
M
T G

D L
?
Q A

64

Which of the following circles' numbers cannot be rearranged into a seven-digit number that is perfectly divisible by 349?

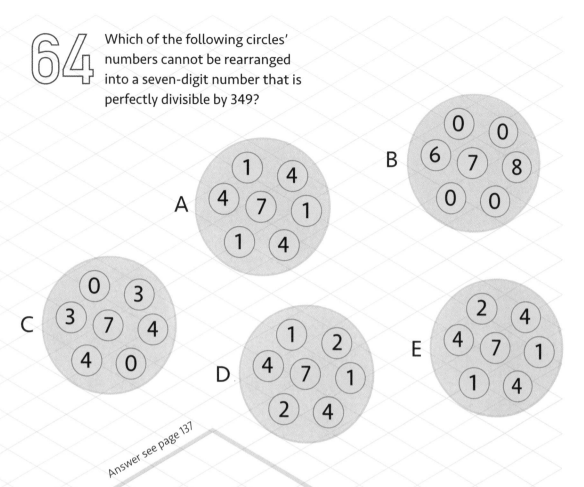

A

B

C

D

E

Answer see page 137

49

65

Can you tell what number comes next in this sequence?

Answer see page 137

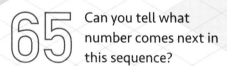

0 1 1 2 3 5 8 ?

Answer see page 137

66

The numbers in the cells represent the number of cells surrounding it that contain mines. Use logic to work out where the mines are placed.

1			2		1		1		1
	2			3				2	2
	1					2	2	3	
		2		2					2
2	2	1	0			2			
						2	1		
	2	1				2		3	
			1		2		1	2	
	3	2				2	2		3
2				2	1				

67

Given the five equations below, what is the value of x?

1. $(4x + 2y) / (a + b) = c$
2. $x^2 + a^2 = c^2 - 2y^2$
3. $3bx = 9y^2$
4. $a + c + 2y = 2b + x$
5. $2x + c = bx + a$

Answer see page 137

68

The numbers on each face of this cube, when arranged correctly, form 8-digit numbers which are the product of 6703 with another four-digit prime number. What are they?

Answer see page 137

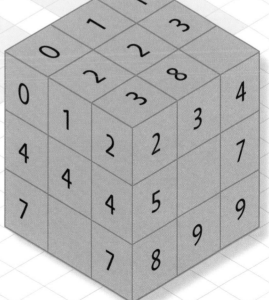

69

A supplier sells boxes of dog biscuits in a range of sizes – 16, 17, 23, 24, 39, and 40 lbs, and will not split boxes. How would you order exactly 100lbs of biscuits?

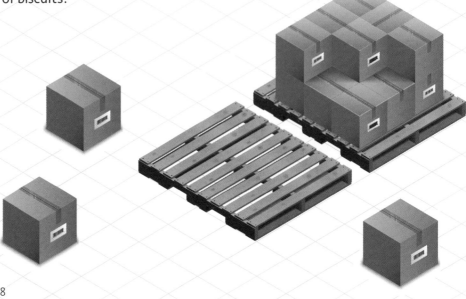

Answer see page 138

70

The following numbers are all types of what?

333336

500500

10011

66066

198765

Answer see page 138

71 According to the logic of these diagrams, what should replace the question mark?

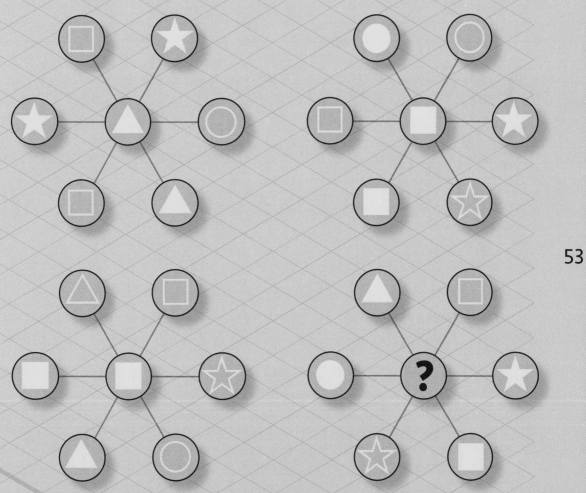

Answer see page 138

72

The word APHIDS is located exactly once in the grid below, but could be horizontally, vertically or diagonally forwards or backwards. Can you locate it?

Answer see page 138

54

H	S	S	P	S	I	S	H	H	S	I	I	A	S	S
S	S	D	D	H	I	I	A	D	P	A	A	D	S	D
A	I	I	A	P	D	H	S	D	A	I	A	A	P	I
I	A	H	P	H	A	I	A	A	P	D	P	P	D
P	D	P	H	H	I	H	D	S	D	D	H	D	I	A
A	P	A	S	P	I	S	I	D	P	P	D	D	A	I
I	P	A	I	D	I	I	A	H	I	A	I	S	I	I
P	I	I	I	I	A	P	D	P	I	S	H	H	P	S
H	A	A	P	D	A	H	I	A	A	A	P	I	H	P
H	D	A	S	I	I	D	D	A	I	A	P	S	P	A
S	A	S	S	D	A	A	S	I	S	S	S	I	H	H
D	A	I	P	P	S	H	I	I	S	H	S	D	S	P
S	D	S	D	A	I	D	I	P	D	A	S	I	D	S
I	A	S	A	I	I	A	A	S	I	A	I	H	P	D
I	P	A	S	D	P	I	D	S	S	S	P	D	I	H

73 This design works according to a specific logic. What should replace the question mark?

? C

7

Y

L

18

Answer see page 138

Answer see page 138

74 Take one letter from each bulb in turn to find five cities. What are they?

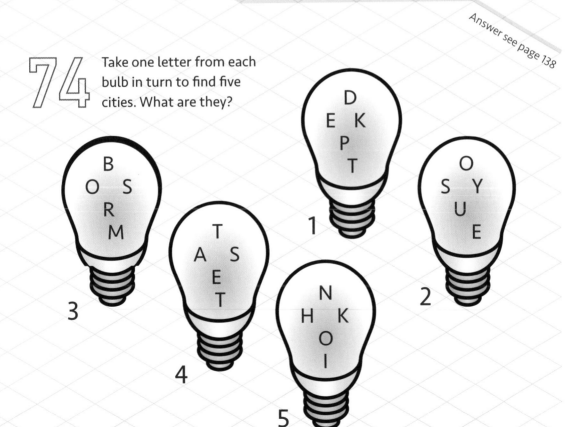

D E K P T

1

O S Y U E

2

B O S R M

3

T A S E T

4

N H K O I

5

75 Following the logic of this grid, what number should replace the question mark?

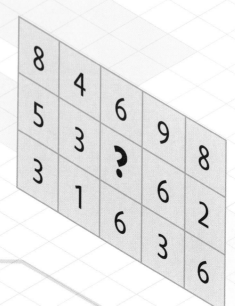

Answer see page 137

76 These triangles follow a certain specific logic. What number should replace the question mark?

Answer see page 138

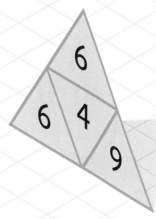

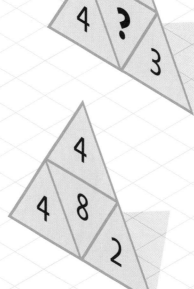

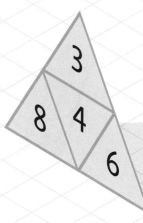

56

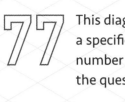

77 This diagram follows a specific logic. What number should replace the question mark?

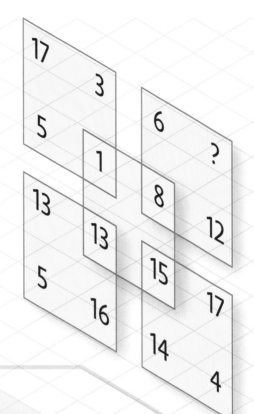

17
3
5
6
?
1
8
13
12
13
15
5
17
16
14
4

Answer see page 138

78 Can you fill in the missing digits to complete this list of square numbers, where each one contains exactly one of the digits 1-9?

Answer see page 138

| 5 | | 8 | | 3 | | 6 | |

| 1 | | 7 | | 9 | | 5 | |

| 5 | | 9 | | 7 | | 8 | |

| 3 | | 9 | | 2 | | 4 | |

| 2 | | 5 | | 7 | | 8 | |

79 The numbers in this diagram, starting at the top and progressing clockwise, represent a valid equation from which all mathematical operators have been removed. Please add back in +, −, * and / signs as necessary to make the equation valid, evaluating each sign's result strictly as you come to it.

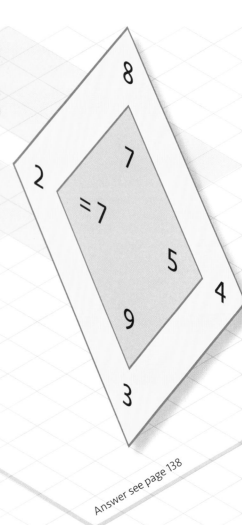

Answer see page 138

58

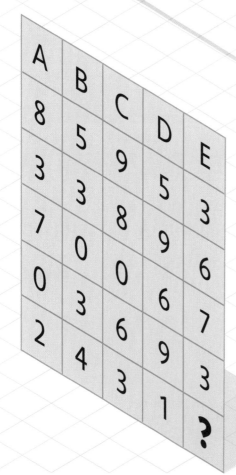

Answer see page 138

80 The following numbers obey a certain logic. What number should replace the question mark?

The symbols in this design appear in a certain order. Which should replace the question mark?

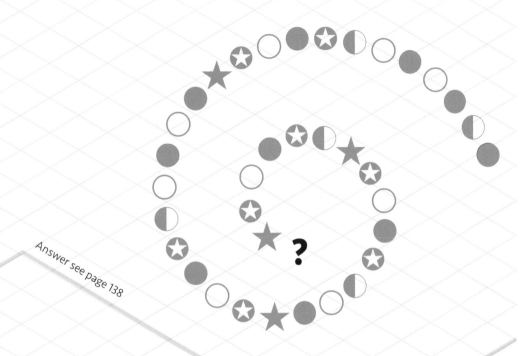

Answer see page 138

Answer see page 138

82 Six of these seven numbers are logically related. Which is the odd one out?

67

43

43

31

35

59

37

83 Logically, which letter in the second circle should be in the first circle?

Answer see page 138

84 This grid obeys a certain logic. What number should replace the question mark?

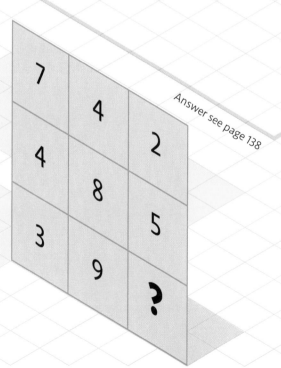

Answer see page 138

85 There are certain numbers missing from this jumbled list. What do they have in common?

54 44 33 34 52 38

39 30 51 36 42 49

40 32 48 35 45 50 46

Answer see page 138

Answer see page 138

86 Following on from the other three clocks, what should be the time on the fourth?

A

B

C

D

87 Four of these five pieces fit together to make a regular geometric shape. Which one is left over?

Answer see page 138

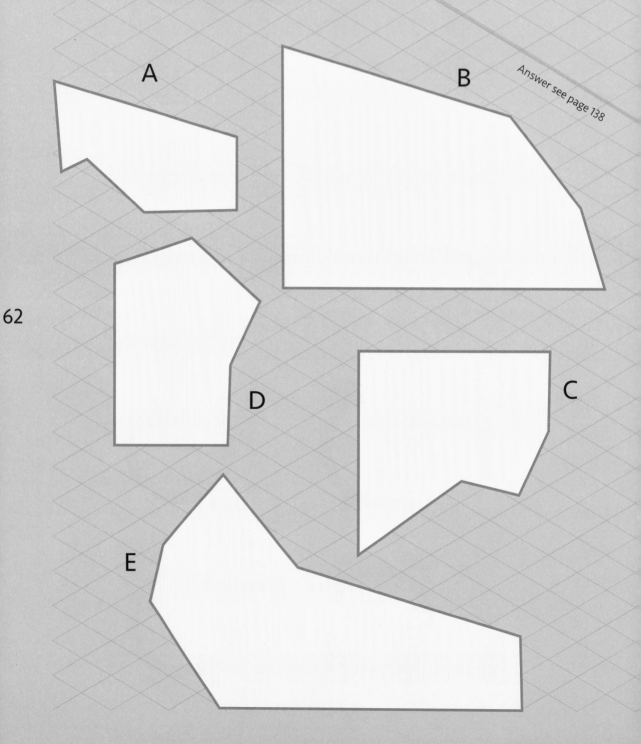

A

B

C

D

E

Can you uncover the logic of this grid
of letters and replace the question
mark with the right letter?

Answer see page 138

Moving from circle to circle without
backtracking, can you find a ten-digit square
number that uses each digit once?

Answer see page 138

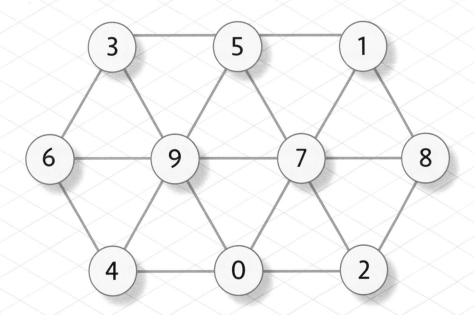

90 The equation spelled out with match-sticks below is correct. Can you move just two matchsticks to form another correct equation?

Answer see page 138

91 The following diagram operates according to a particular logic. Which letter should replace the question mark?

Answer see page 138

92 These circles function according to a certain logic. What number should replace the question mark?

B

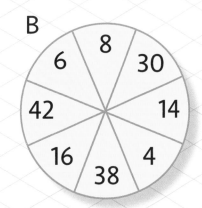

8
6
30
42
14
16
4
38

A

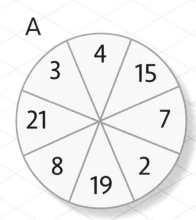

4
3
15
21
7
8
2
19

C

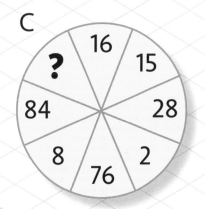

16
?
15
84
28
8
2
76

Answer see page 138

65

93 All the mathematical symbols have been removed from this balanced equation. Can you reconstitute it?

Answer see page 138

23 ◯ 8 ◯ 1 ◯ 10 ◯ 5 ◯ 8 ◯ 2 ◯ 1

Which pair of sides
contain the same
roman numbers?

Answer see page 138

66

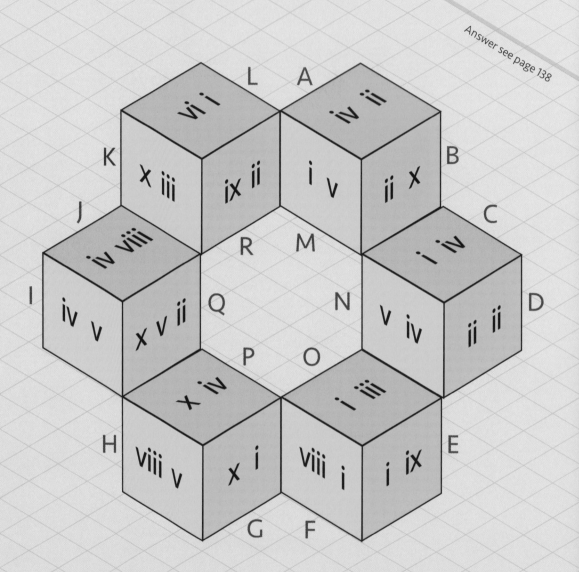

95 What is the missing number?

Answer see page 139

Answer see page 138

96 There is a pattern behind these dominoes. What should replace the question mark?

97 Either multiplying or dividing by a single digit integer each time, and making sure each result is between 0 and 9999, can you get from the top number to the bottom number using precisely three intermediate steps?

1	0	2	4
2	6	8	8

Answer see page 139

Answer see page 139

98 How many circles are in this congeries?

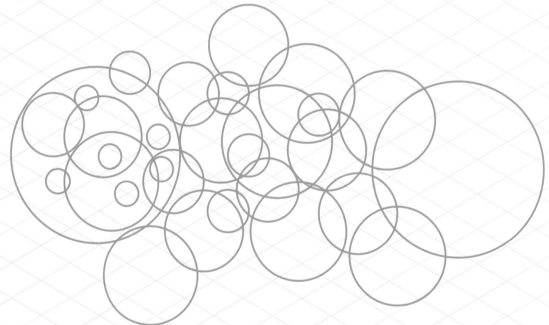

Answer see page 139

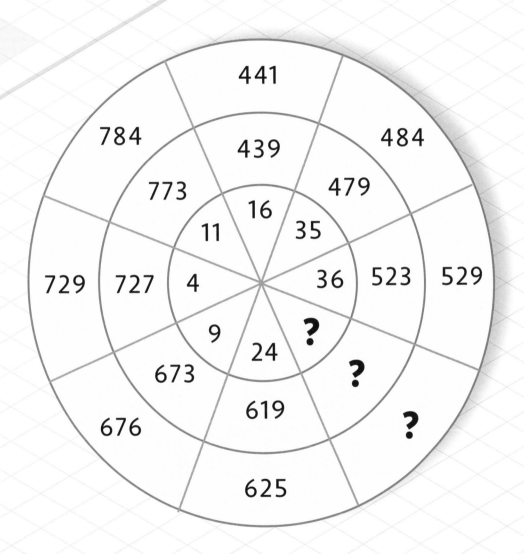

441
784
439
484
773
479
16
11
35
729 727 4
36 523 529
9
24
?
673
?
619
676
?
625

99 In the above diagram, what number should replace the question marks?

100

The dots on this grid have been filled according to a specific logic. One filled dot has been left out. Where should it go?

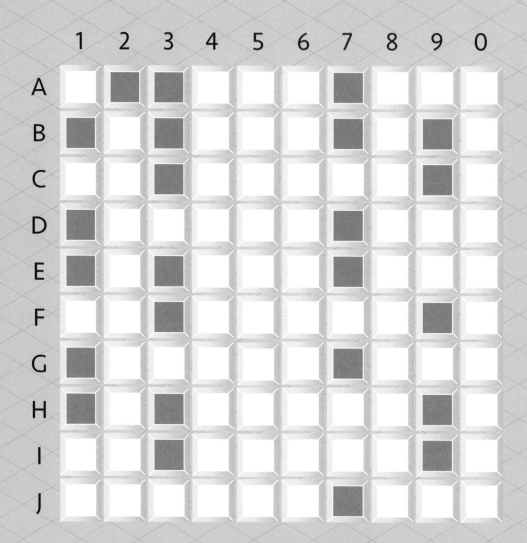

70

Answer see page 139

101

The numbers in this list are sequential terms in a specific sequence of numbers, but they are out of order. What is the sequence?

121393
1346269
196418
2178309
317811
3524578
46368
514229
75025
832040

Answer see page 139

Answer see page 139

102

The Roman numeral equation spelled out with match-sticks below is incorrect. Can you move just one matchstick to form a correct equation?

Answer see page 139

2R	3DR	3D	1DR	4DL	6D	4DL
1UR	4D	1DL	2L	1R	4D	6L
5R	2UR	4DR	1UL	3D	1D	2U
3U	1D	1U	F	1U	2UL	5L
2U	1DL	4R	1R	4U	1UR	3U
1D	2UR	2UL	3U	2L	1R	3U
4R	1R	1UR	2U	3L	2U	3L

103

Each square on this grid shows you the move you must make to arrive at the next square in the sequence, Left, Right, Up, and/or Down. So 3R would be three squares right, and 4UL would be 4 squares diagonally up and left. Your goal is to end up on the finish square, F, having visited every square exactly once. Can you find the starting square?

104 These circles obey a certain logic. Knowing that, what letter should replace the question mark?

Answer see page 139

Answer see page 139

105 These dominos obey a certain logic. What should replace the question mark?

$\dfrac{H}{H}$ $\dfrac{L}{B}$ $\dfrac{B}{C}$ $\dfrac{N}{O}$ $\dfrac{F}{?}$

106

Delete all instances of letters that appear more than once, and rearrange the remainder to find the name of a city. What is it?

E	P	L	A	D	Q	S	X
F	P	L	T	I	H	G	H
M	N	Y	T	I	H	B	W
Q	J	G	Z	X	O	U	C
D	K	R	O	I	X	F	F
J	X	S	V	M	K	Y	B

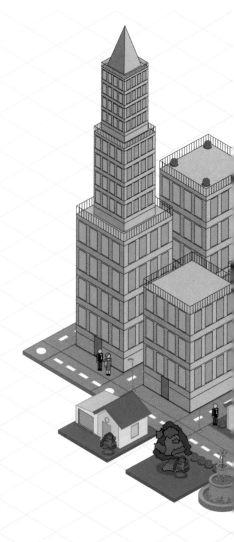

Answer see page 139

107

In the irregular magic square below, every row, column and five-figure diagonal adds to 115. The blank spaces below each need to be filled by one of four numbers. Can you complete the square?

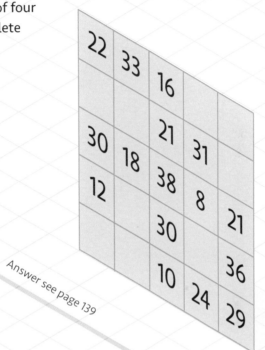

Answer see page 139

108

This design works according to a specific logic. What should replace the question mark?

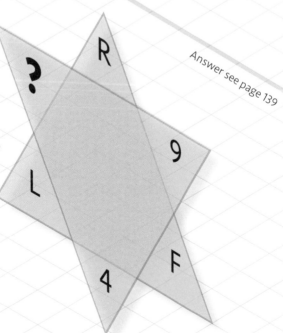

Answer see page 139

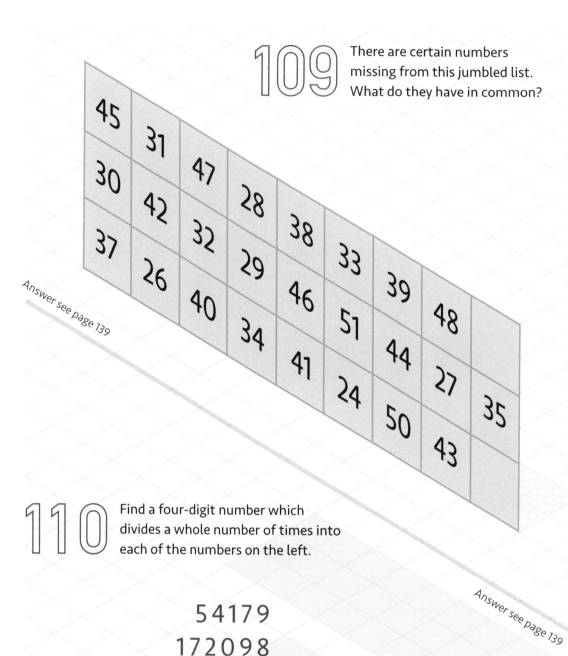

109 There are certain numbers missing from this jumbled list. What do they have in common?

45 31 47 30 28 42 38 32 37 33 29 26 39 46 40 51 48 34 44 41 27 24 35 50 43

110 Find a four-digit number which divides a whole number of times into each of the numbers on the left.

54179
172098
6374
82862
270895
73301

111 The following diagram obeys a specific logic. What should replace the question mark?

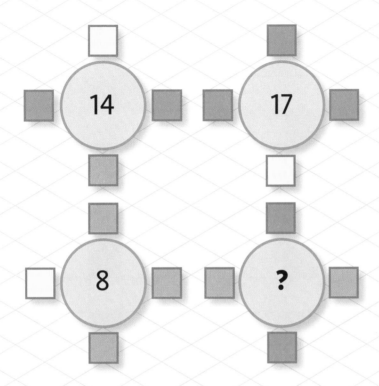

14   17

8   ?

Answer see page 139

Answer see page 139

112 You have a coin that is biased, and does not generate heads and tails with equal probability. How can you use it to make an unbiased either/or decision?

Can you fill in the numbers provided to correctly complete the grid?

Answer see page 140

78

3 digit numbers	420	4 digit numbers	7 digit numbers	9 digit numbers
183	483	3327	1277149	168357562
212	534	6433		233571289
256	584	8021	8 digit numbers	391368944
301	598			596682946
342	619	6 digit numbers	84332386	860352417
374	660		89239583	974132425
376	876	266447		
409	933	749394		
	972			

114

This grid obeys a specific sequence. However, some numbers are out of order. When shaded in, these will reveal another number. What is it?

6	3	8	0	1	2	5	0	3
1	4	3	6	3	8	2	5	2
5	1	4	1	4	3	6	3	5
0	1	0	5	0	3	1	4	3
6	3	5	0	1	2	5	0	4
1	4	3	6	3	8	0	1	0
5	0	4	1	4	0	6	3	1
0	1	0	5	0	3	0	6	0
6	3	1	0	1	2	5	0	6
1	4	3	6	3	8	0	1	0
5	0	4	1	4	0	6	3	1
0	1	0	5	0	3	1	4	3
6	0	1	0	1	2	4	5	3
1	4	0	6	3	8	0	1	2

115 Two moons are orbiting a planet. One takes 16 days to make a full circuit. The other takes 9 days. If they are now in a perfect conjunction, with the quicker moon directly in between the planet and the slower moon, when will the three celestial bodies next be in a straight line?

Answer see page 140

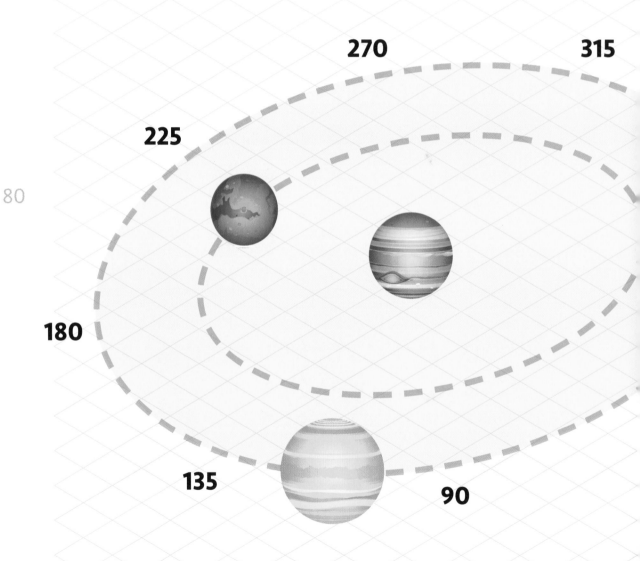

270

315

225

180

135

90

116

The letters on this cube, when correctly assembled, spell out the name of a novel and its author. What is it?

Answer see page 140

Answer see page 140

0

81

117

These triangles obey a certain logic. What letter should replace the question mark?

5

118

Can you fill in the missing digits to complete this list of square numbers, where each one contains exactly one of the digits 1-9?

	2	9	3	8	
	4	1	9	3	
	2	1	7	5	
	1	3	4	7	
	3	2	9	8	

Answer see page 140

119

What should replace the question mark in the final square?

Answer see page 140

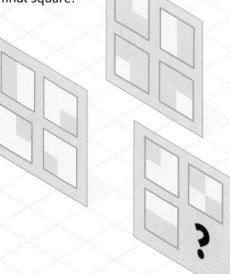
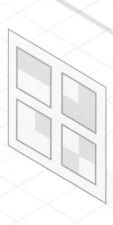

120 Examine the following sets of scales, which are in perfect balance. How many squares are needed to balance the final scale?

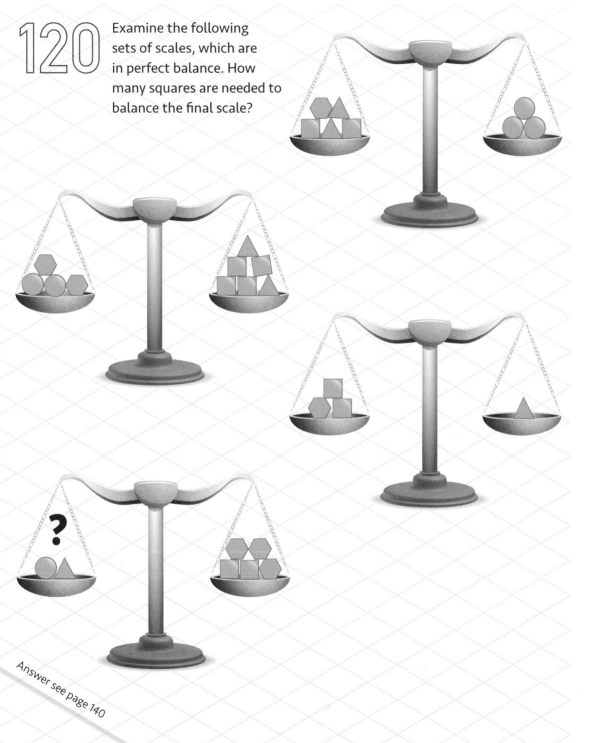

Answer see page 140

Answer see page 140

121

The numbers in the cells represent the number of cells surrounding it that contain mines. Use logic to work out where the mines are placed.

1			2			4			
	3	3	3		3	3	4	2	2
					2				
		3	3	2		1			
2								2	
0		2	2			0	2		2
		1	1				2	3	
1						0	0		
2	3			1				3	
	3		2			1	1	3	2
		3	3					4	2
	2	0		2	1			2	

122 Which of the following circles' numbers cannot be rearranged into a seven-digit number that is perfectly divisible by 523?

Answer see page 140

Answer see page 140

123 All the mathematical symbols have been removed from this balanced equation. Can you reconstitute it?

13 ◯ 5 ◯ 6 ◯ 4 ◯ 16 ◯ 6 ◯ 2 ◯ 8 ◯ 4

These triangles follow a certain specific logic. What number should replace the question mark?

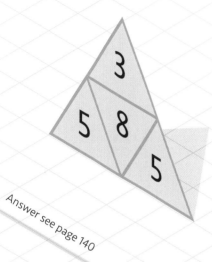

Answer see page 140

Answer see page 140

125 What weight will balance the beam?

126

These numbers, when placed correctly into the grid, will give you two numbers which are multiples of the number 84337. Can you disentangle them?

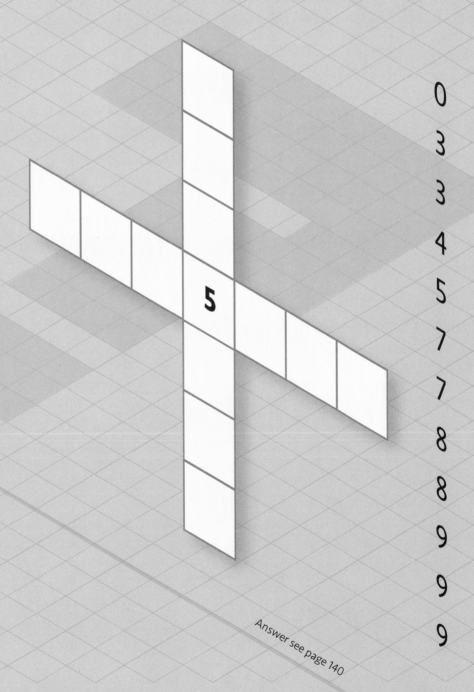

5

0
3
3
4
5
7
7
8
8
9
9

Answer see page 140

127

Which of the four options A-D below most closely matches the conditions of the top figure?

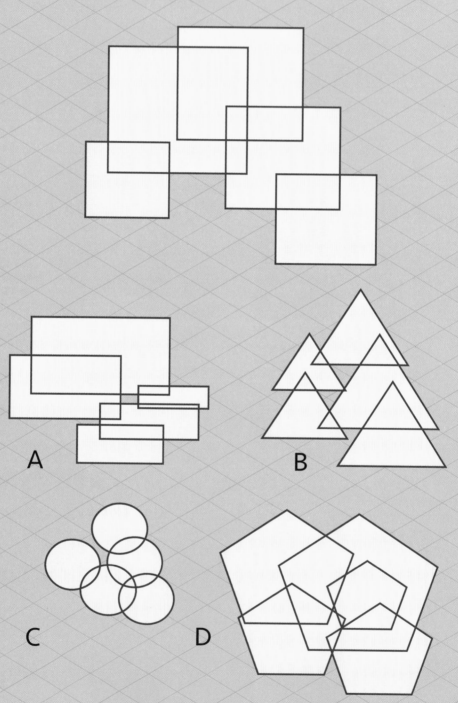

A

B

C

D

88

Which of the shapes below, A-E,
fits with the shape above to form a
perfect dark octagon?

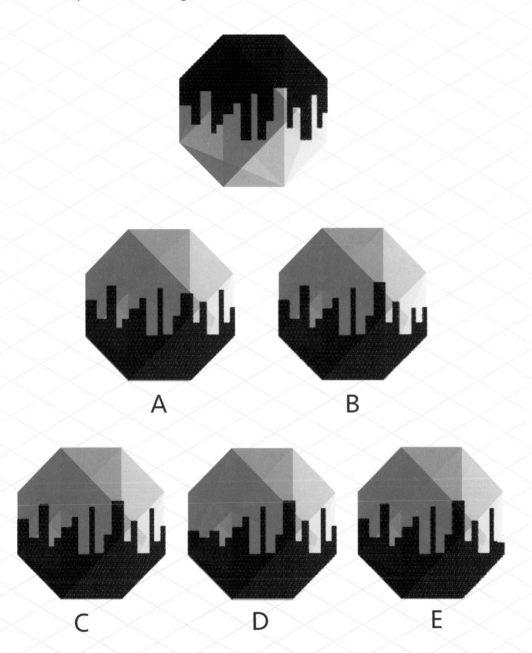

A

B

C

D

E

Answer see page 141

129

Several famous paintings have
been encoded using the key below.
Can you decipher them?

1	2	3	4	5	6	7	8	9
a	b	c	d	e	f	g	h	i
j	k	l	m	n	o	p	q	r
s	t	u	v	w	x	y	z	

7	9	3	1	5	7	7	5	9	1	9	3	9	4	2	6	3	4	6	9	2	8	5	9	6	9	9	5	

4	1	6	9	2	5	3	2	4	1	5	5	9	1	3	2	6	9	1	9	2	9	9	7	2	7	3	8	

6	9	9	2	1	9	4	1	5	9	4	5	5	9	2	5	9	7	8	5	9	1	3	5	4	1	7		

6	9	1	5	3	9	1	3	6	9	7	6	7	1	9	3	1	9	5	9	4	1	3	9	1	3	5	5	5

4	9	5	3	5	5	2	9	4	1	5	9	7	6	7	8	9	1	5	3	6	7	6	9	2	9	1	9	2

90

Answer see page 141

Answer see page 141

130

Following the logic of
this grid, what number
should replace the
question mark?

3	4	3	
1	9	3	2
7	1	9	7
2	7	2	?

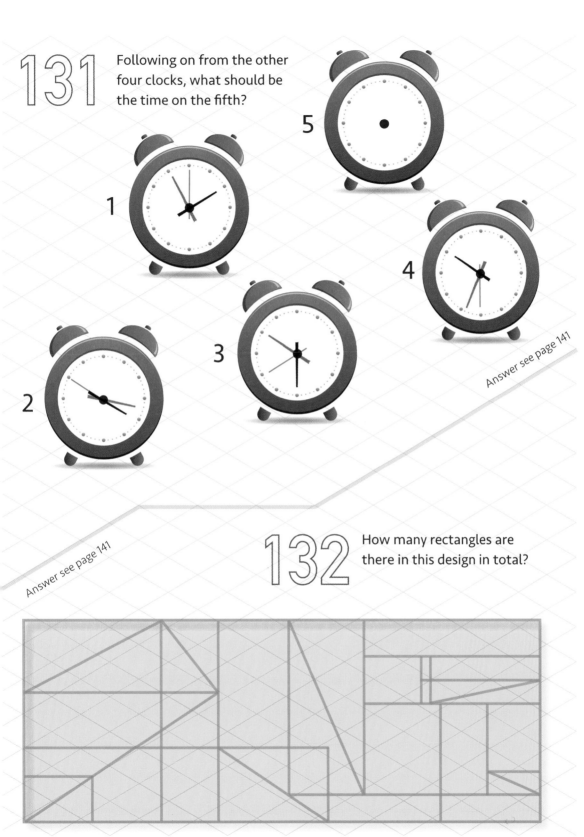

131

Following on from the other four clocks, what should be the time on the fifth?

1

2

3

4

5

Answer see page 141

Answer see page 141

132

How many rectangles are there in this design in total?

133 Signs – symbols in a specific position – which appear in the outer circles are transferred to the inner circle as follows: If it appears once or thrice, it is definitely transferred. If it appears twice, it is transferred if no other symbol will be transferred. If it appears four times, it is not transferred.

What does the inner circle look like?

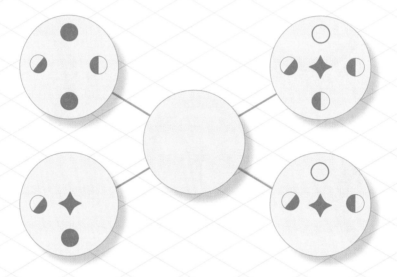

Answer see page 141

Answer see page 141

134 Starting at one corner and spiralling around to end on the centre square, you will find a nine-letter word. Two of the letters are missing. What is it?

135

The following list of numbers represents creatures whose letters have been encoded into the numbers needed to reproduce them on a typical phone numberpad. Can you decode them?

Answer see page 141

262 266 32

424 7

324 436 2

783 892 5

268 328 37

136

Four of these five pieces fit together to make a regular geometric shape. Which one is left over?

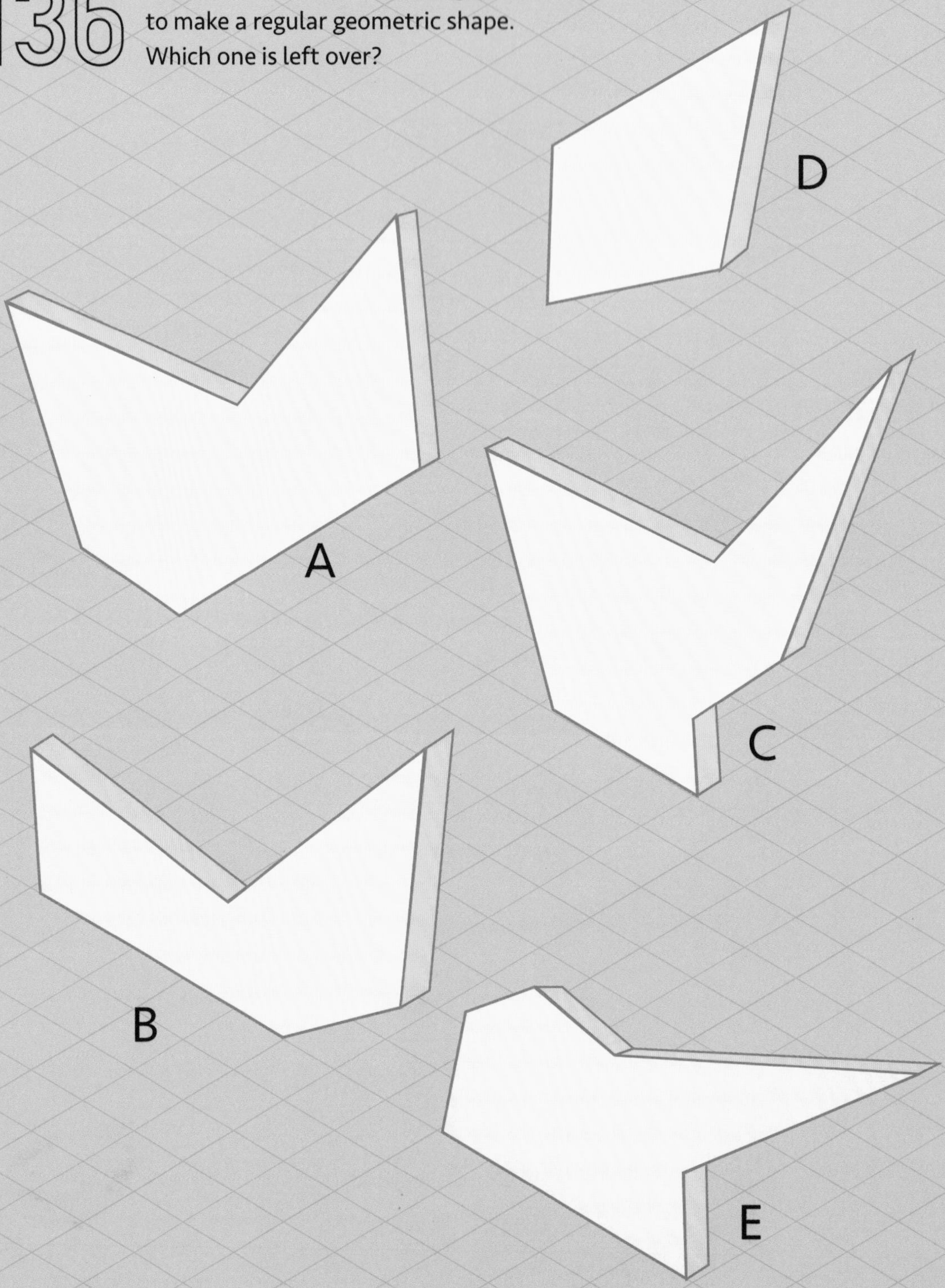

A

B

C

D

E

137

The following numbers obey a certain logic. What number should replace the question mark?

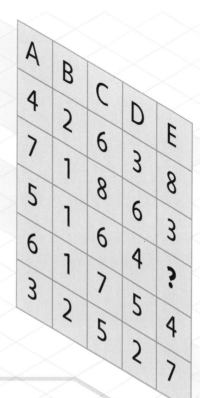

A	B	C	D	E
4	2	6	3	
7	1		3	8
5	1	8	6	8
6	1	6	4	3
3	2	7	5	?
		5	2	4
				7

Answer see page 141

138

The symbols in this design appear in a certain order. Which should replace the question mark?

Answer see page 141

139

Which of these is the odd one out?

A: WILSON

B: DOUGLAS-HOME

C: ATTLEE

D: KINNOCK

E: ASQUITH

F: BALFOUR

G: MACDONALD

Answer see page 141

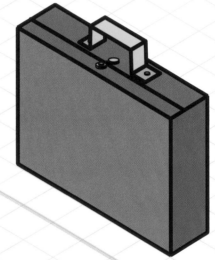

140

What is the missing number?

Answer see page 141

141

The numbers in this list are sequential terms in a specific sequence of numbers, but the numbers in the right hand column have been scrambled. What is the sequence?

1 3 3 3 4 4 4	5 5 6 7 7 7 7
1 3 3 3 4 5	5 5 7 7 8
1 3 4 4 4	6 6 6 6 7 7
1 3 4 5	6 6 7 7
1 4 5	6 6 8
1 6	7 7

97

Answer see page 141

Answer see page 141

142

What is special about the integer

8,549,176,320

that is not true of any other specific positive integer?

Answer see page 141

143

Which of the following numbers is not a numerical anagram of 93426151821685832045?

a. 12429311460825685538

b. 26484235258110396851

c. 35911246838860214552

d. 08926155228814465132

e. 89836550418215132426

f. 82563135415849680212

g. 35622882145386150941

h. 82563293615240158148

i. 56065134815221432988

144 What single letter is missing from all four grids?

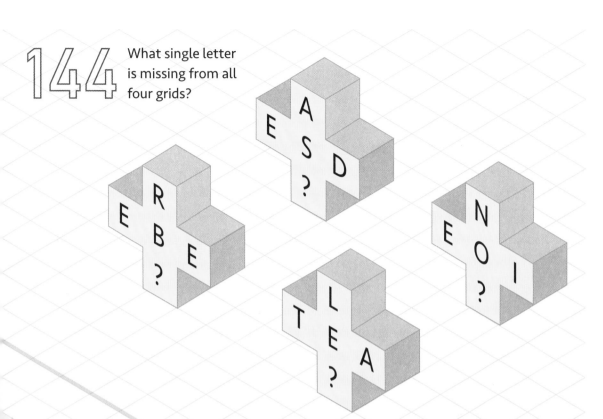

Answer see page 141

Answer see page 141

145 The following diagram operates according to a particular logic. Which letter should replace the question mark?

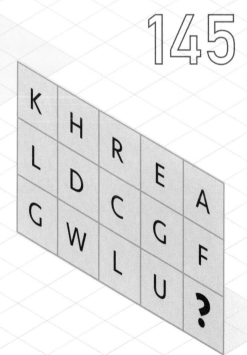

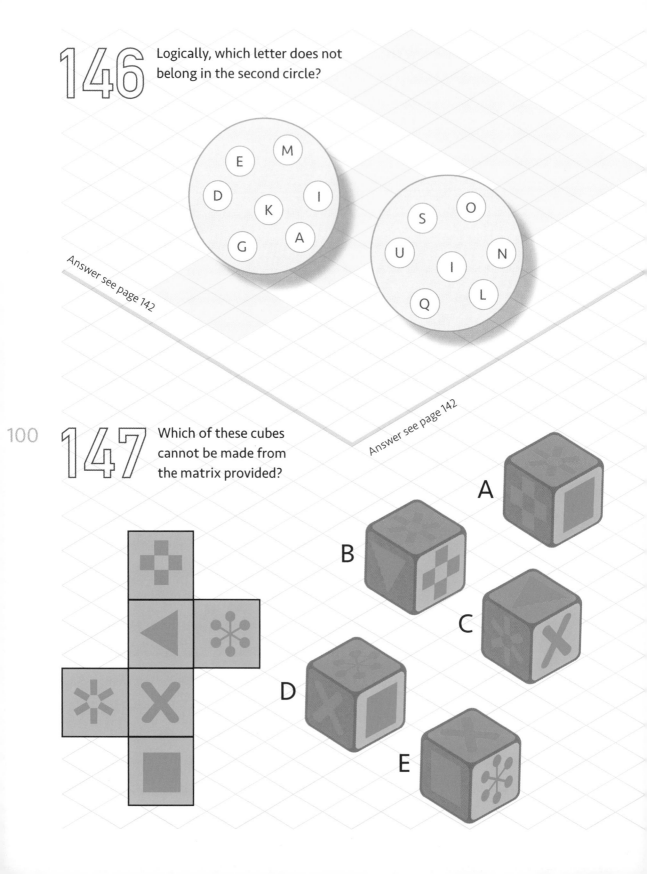

146 Logically, which letter does not belong in the second circle?

Answer see page 142

147 Which of these cubes cannot be made from the matrix provided?

Answer see page 142

148

The following tiles have been taken from a five by five square of numbers. When they have been reassembled accurately, the square will show the same five numbers reading both across and down.

Can you rebuild it?

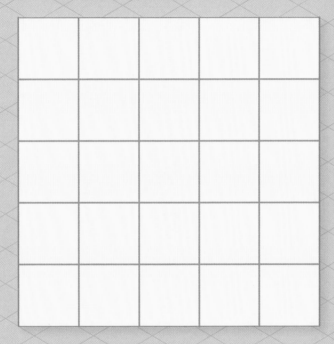

| 1 | 1 | 9 |

| 2 | 7 | 6 |

| 0 |
| 1 |
| 8 |

| 8 |
| 4 |
| 2 |

| 4 |
| 3 |
| 1 |

| 1 | 5 | 9 |

| 7 |
| 6 |

| 9 | 0 | 2 | 5 | 1 | 8 |

Answer see page 142

149

The dots on this grid have been filled according to a specific logic. One filled dot has been left out. Where should it go?

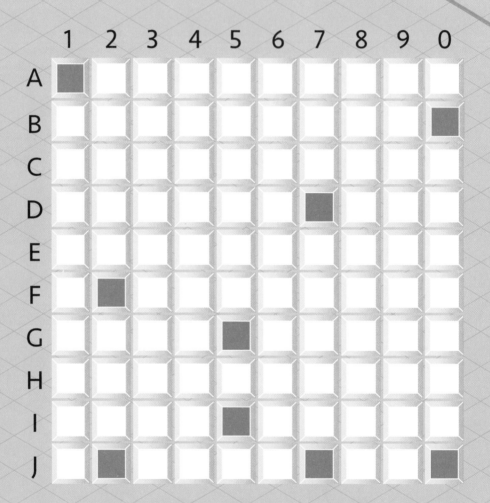

Answer see page 142

150

When the following grid is completed correctly, it will contain six different numbers that can follow 893 to produce a six-digit number that has 149 as a divisor.

Answer see page 142

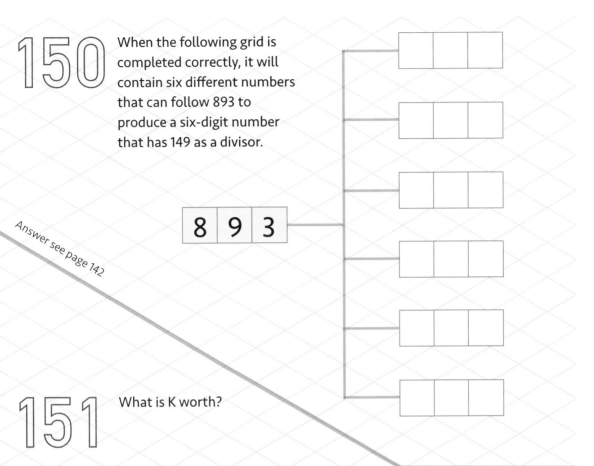

8 9 3

151

What is K worth?

Answer see page 142

$K + K + N = 42$

$L + M + N = 34$

$K + M + N = 29$

$L + N + L = 52$

152 If Amanda supports the Tigers, Bridget supports the Rhinos, and Taylor supports the Elks, Who does Annie support?

a. The Leopards

b. The Bulldogs

c. The Human Beings

d. The Moose

e. The Antelopes

Answer see page 142

Answer see page 142

153 Each symbol in the grid has a consistent value. What number should replace the question mark?

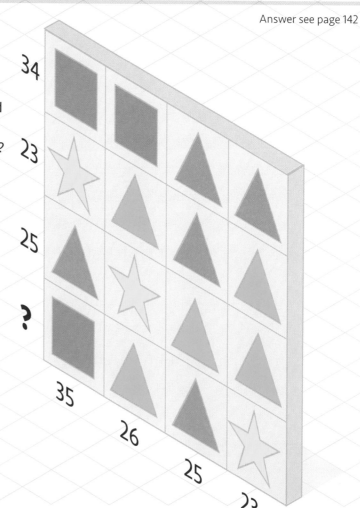

34

23

25

?

35

26

25

23

154

The numbers in this diagram, starting at the top and progressing clockwise, represent a valid equation from which all mathematical operators have been removed. Please add back in +, −, * and / signs as necessary to make the equation valid, evaluating each sign's result strictly as you come to it.

9

23

5

= 7

2

7

8

18

Answer see page 142

155

These circles function according to a certain logic. What number should replace the question mark?

Answer see page 142

156 One of the squares in the 3x3 grid is incorrect. Which one?

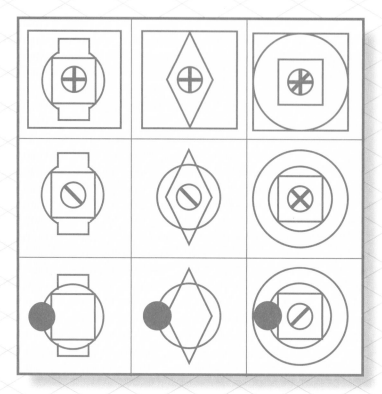

Answer see page 142

Answer see page 142

157 Which letter is one to the right of the letter four to the right of the letter one to the right of the letter two to the left of the letter two to the left of the letter immediately towards the middle of the line from the letter three to the right of the letter two to the right of the letter E?

158

Using only numbers available in the grid below, subtract the largest Mersenne number from the number with the most divisors. What is the result?

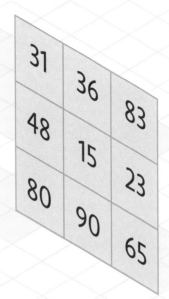

31	36	83
48	15	23
80	90	65

Answer see page 142

159

You have 56 biscuits to feed to your ten pets, which are made up of some cats and some dogs. Dogs get 6 biscuits, while cats get 5. You finish with one biscuit remaining. How many cats and how many dogs do you have?

Answer see page 142

160

Can you find the 36 numbers shown below within the number grid?

9	7	4	9	5	6	7	0	1	3	6	9	8	1	6
0	7	1	1	2	9	0	0	0	8	4	6	9	3	2
9	8	2	1	4	3	7	6	0	9	9	2	7	3	9
6	9	4	5	0	5	5	7	2	0	2	2	7	5	7
0	3	1	9	5	9	8	6	9	4	7	8	9	1	3
4	3	1	6	2	5	3	2	2	1	9	2	4	3	3
6	9	8	0	9	6	9	2	0	4	8	4	2	7	7
6	1	1	8	9	8	4	5	9	0	5	0	0	1	8
9	6	5	1	5	7	8	9	7	1	2	8	3	4	7
0	8	7	3	7	5	0	7	8	4	2	1	6	0	0
8	1	9	3	1	8	2	6	0	7	8	6	6	3	9
9	5	1	5	4	1	4	8	6	8	0	8	0	9	1
6	6	7	1	9	6	6	4	8	5	1	8	9	2	3
3	1	5	1	1	6	9	3	2	3	7	9	2	3	8
5	1	9	3	5	5	2	5	6	0	0	4	6	0	0

270	11513	525600	29122352
277	37926	789462	66406909
422	40392	968959	79420366
1377	68414	2143760	87091380
2048	69809	4660525	112900084
2258	75505	4802469	124118157
4898	180788	5193552	622824081
5962	351371	9853956	749567013
9927	488930	15148099	861933987

Answer see page 142

Which is the odd
one out?

A

B

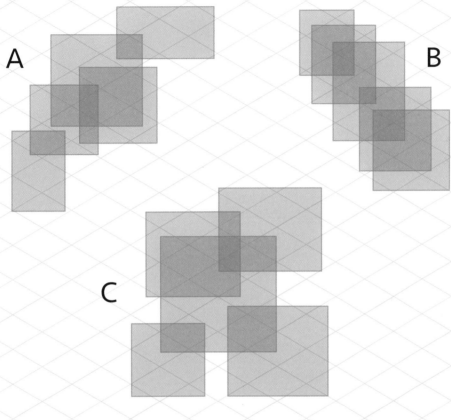

C

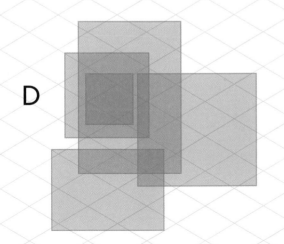

D

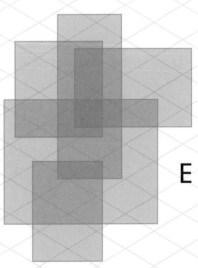

E

109

Answer see page 142

162

The following terms are all anagrams of mountains. Can you disentangle them?

CLONE TUMMY INK

OMAN JAIL IRK

AEROBIC ZIP ADO

TOP PEACE PLOT

DUB MACHINE

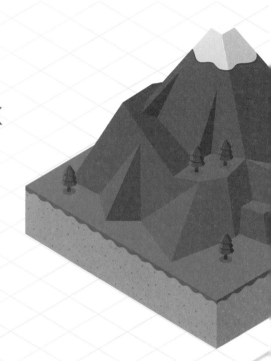

Answer see page 142

Answer see page 142

163

Either multiplying or dividing by a single digit integer each time, and making sure each result is between 0 and 9999, can you get from the top number to the bottom number using precisely three intermediate steps?

1	3	4	4
1	9	6	0

164

Can you tell what number comes next in this sequence?

1   2   5   10   17   26   ?

Answer see page 143

Answer see page 143

165

Moving from circle to circle without backtracking, can you find a ten-digit square number that uses each digit once?

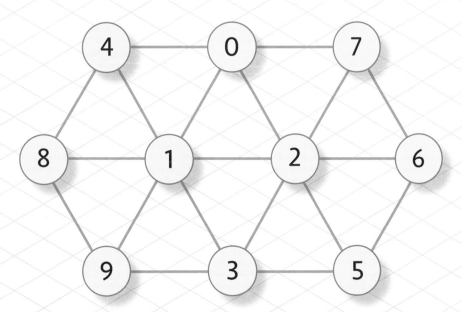

166

These pairs of circles obey a certain logic. What letter should replace the question mark?

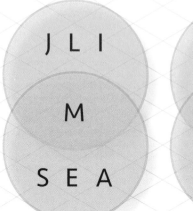
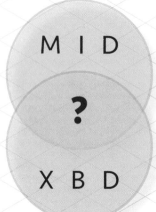

Answer see page 143

167

These suitcases are shown with their destinations. Which is the odd one out?

Answer see page 143

Australia

Corfu

Borneo

Dodecanese

Elba

168

Which trio of sides contain the same roman numbers?

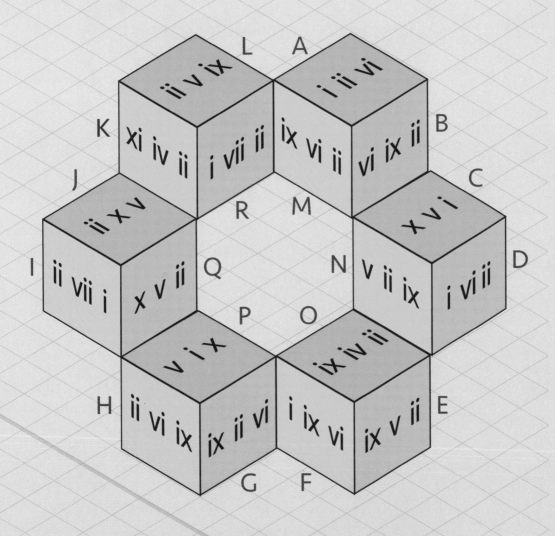

Answer see page 143

169 Six of these seven numbers are logically related. Which is the odd one out?

(28) (14) (55) (46) (82) (64) (41)

Answer see page 143

Answer see page 143

170 Starting at any corner, follow the paths until you have five numbers, including the one where you started. Do not backtrack. Add the five together. What is the highest number you can obtain?

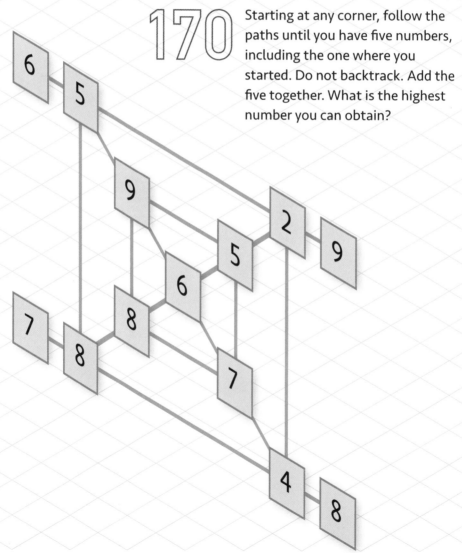

114

171

These rings obey a certain logic. What number should replace the question mark?

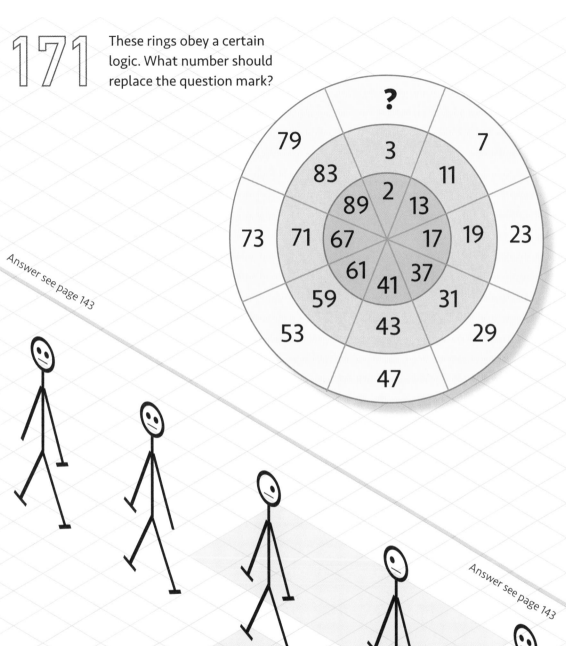

Answer see page 143

Answer see page 143

172

What would the next matchstick person in this sequence look like?

173 Can you find the square which contains the number in this grid that is 3 squares from itself plus seven, 4 squares from itself minus thirteen, 5 squares from itself plus three, and 3 squares from itself minus two? All distances are in straight lines.

Answer see page 143

	a	b	c	d	e	f	g	h	i
1	14	48	96	28	98	74	41	40	92
2	40	84	52	95	17	84	25	29	65
3	85	18	77	20	28	54	81	22	7
4	17	86	9	30	84	67	20	56	80
5	29	55	4	66	32	17	29	60	11
6	33	18	84	25	12	52	78	41	61
7	36	41	12	49	20	70	12	24	98
8	57	27	89	94	25	35	64	22	12
9	75	58	35	61	23	83	39	52	68

Can you arrange the following twelve numbers into four groups of three related numbers each?

44	121	421
100	144	440
101	211	441
111	222	444

Answer see page 143

Answer see page 143

The following design works according to a certain logic. What number should replace the question mark?

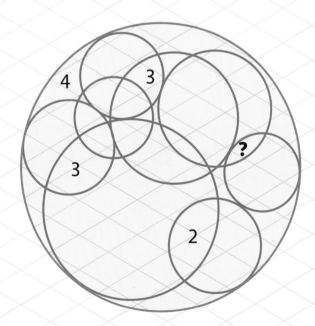

176

The following five items are all famous lakes. Can you decrypt them?

BDYNARXA   NARN

VRLQRPJW   XWCJARX

QDAXW

Answer see page 143

Answer see page 143

177

This non-pandigital grid obeys a certain logic. What number should replace the question mark?

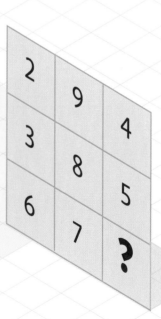

This design follows a specific logic. What should replace the question mark

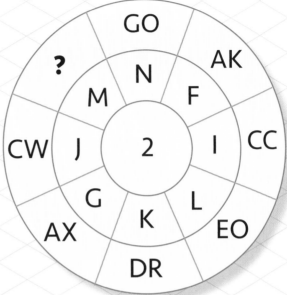

Answer see page 143

18 A
S

T ?
O

T
19 I
N
L 1

Answer see page 143

179

The letters and numbers in this square obey a certain logic. What number should replace the question mark?

According to the logic of these diagrams, what should replace the question mark?

Answer see page 143

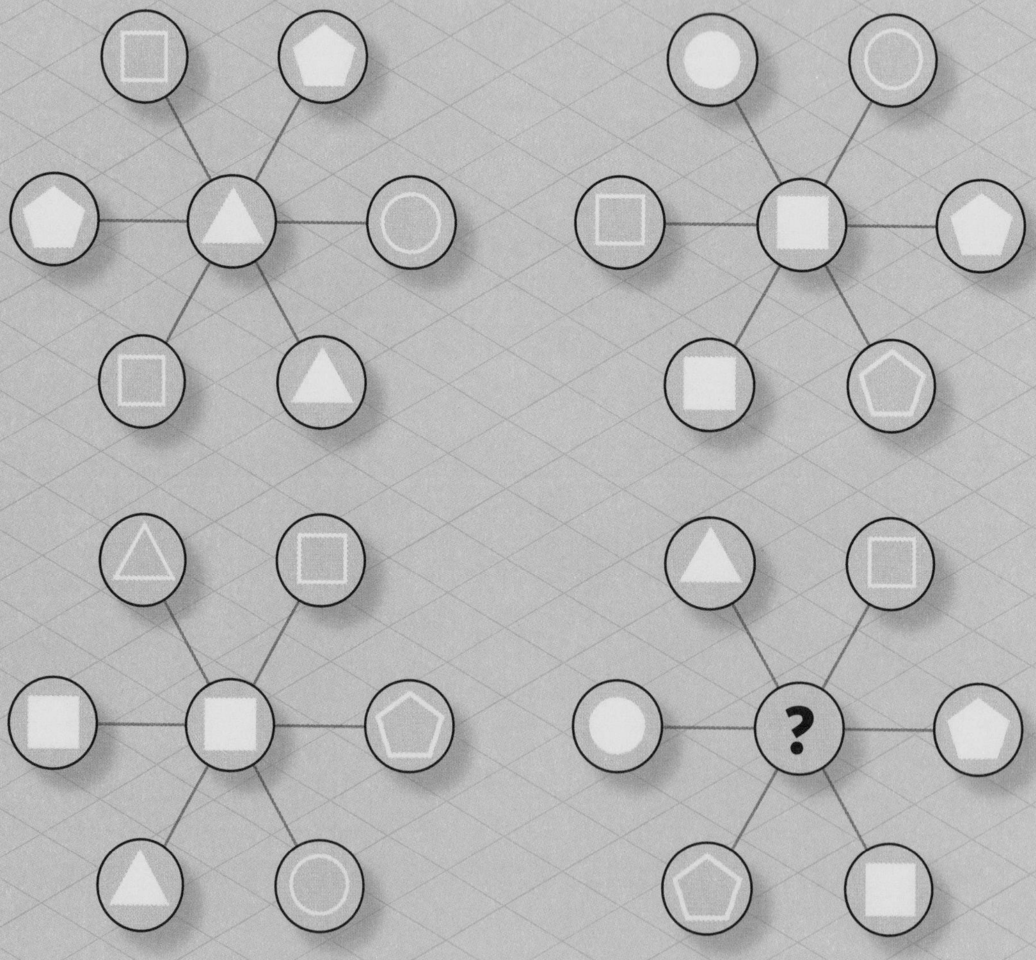

120

181

There is a similarity between the two circles. Knowing that, what number should replace the question mark?

Answer see page 143

Answer see page 143

182

How many circles are in this congeries?

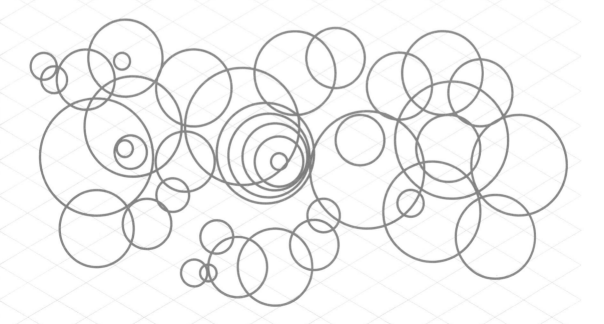

183

Which of the following is not an anagram of a type of cheese?

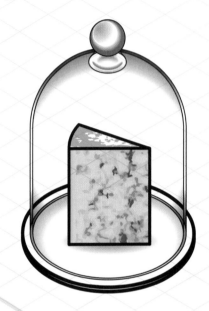

FOR TORQUE

YOWLS MELD

BATCH MINER

MEMBER CAT

NEWLY-SEALED

RICE LED RESET

Answer see page 143

Answer see page 143

184

Four 4-digit square numbers are jumbled in this square. Which pair of numbers is not used?

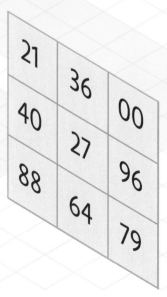

21	36	
40		00
	27	96
88	64	
		79

185

Figure A is to figure B as figure C is to which figure?

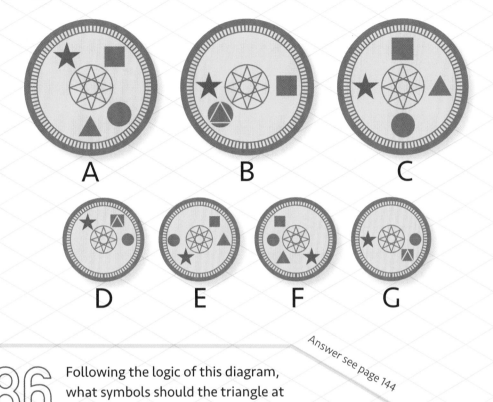

A   B   C

D   E   F   G

Answer see page 144

186

Following the logic of this diagram, what symbols should the triangle at the top contain?

Answer see page 144

187 The numbers in this list are sequential terms in a specific sequence of numbers, but they are out of order. What is the sequence?

999999999989

9973

99999999977

99999989

99991

9999999967

99999999999971

999983

999999937

9999991

Answer see page 144

Answer see page 144

188 Given the five equations below, what is the value of x?

1. $3x^2 - x = b(ca + 2yb)$

2. $4b / 3 = c$

3. $a - x = c - by$

4. $(2x / 3)c = 2a + 2y$

5. $x + y = ay$

Answer see page 144

189

The word LUMINOUS is located exactly once in the grid below, but could be horizontally, vertically or diagonally forwards or backwards. Can you locate it?

O	S	N	S	I	O	M	S	S	I	O	N	I	U	I
L	U	S	U	M	U	N	U	S	U	L	U	U	O	N
M	U	N	O	I	S	N	U	M	L	U	S	L	N	S
S	O	I	S	U	O	O	L	U	N	S	L	S	O	I
I	U	U	L	M	U	L	U	M	I	U	L	S	U	N
L	M	S	U	M	N	M	N	U	S	I	S	M	I	O
S	N	U	I	N	I	I	S	I	M	L	O	M	U	S
I	M	I	U	I	U	L	O	U	L	I	L	M	O	N
I	N	O	O	S	U	O	N	I	M	U	L	S	N	N
M	U	O	N	U	L	O	O	U	U	U	O	L	M	U
O	N	U	S	I	U	L	O	M	S	M	S	N	I	L
L	U	M	U	U	I	S	M	L	I	U	N	M	O	L
L	O	U	M	M	I	S	I	U	N	U	S	S	S	I
I	L	N	O	O	I	O	L	O	O	S	L	N	M	O
N	N	L	L	I	L	S	O	O	M	S	U	U	O	I

In the following diagram, what number should replace the question marks?

Answer see page 144

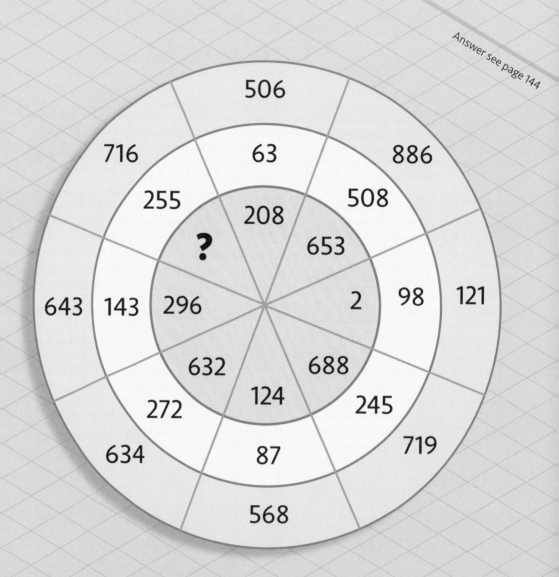

191

Can you work out the answer to this quick riddle?
What gets wetter the more it dries?

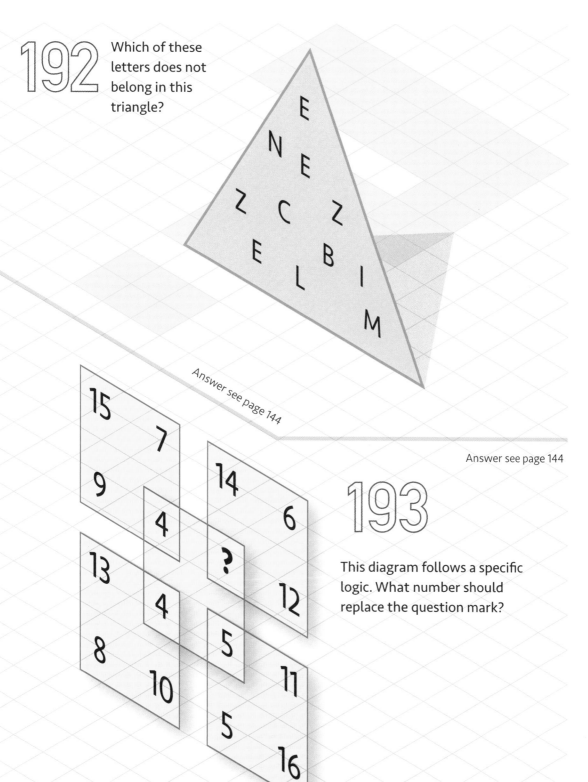

192 Which of these letters does not belong in this triangle?

E
N E
Z C Z
E B
L I
M

Answer see page 144

15
7
9
4
13
4
8
10

14
6
?
12
5
11
5
16

Answer see page 144

193

This diagram follows a specific logic. What number should replace the question mark?

Find a three-digit number which divides a whole number of times into each of the numbers on the left.

33535

313111

73777 ☐ ☐ ☐

29299

3883

Answer see page 144

Answer see page 144

195 Taking a letter from each ball in turn, can you spell out three different world cities?

OIL

MVL

LIE

EOE

WLD

NRM

DIE

STB

LAV

TIE

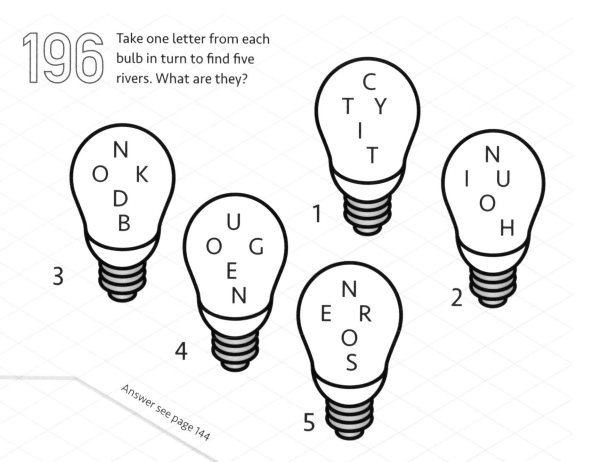

196 Take one letter from each bulb in turn to find five rivers. What are they?

1

2

3

4

5

129

Answer see page 144

197 A committee of five needs to be drawn from twelve people, five men and seven women. There must be at least two women and one man. How many different ways of doing this are there?

198

There is a pattern behind these dominoes. What should replace the question mark?

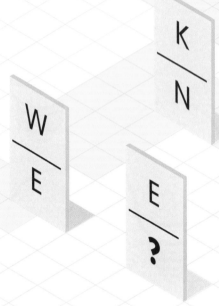

K / N

W / E

O / T

E / ?

Answer see page 144

130

Answer see page 144

199

There is something wrong with this list. Can you tell what it is?

Biscay

Chesapeake

James

Hudson

Ionian

Baffin

Bengal

Fundy

Campeche

Can you find your
way through this
maze?

START

FINISH

Answer see page 144

The following grid operates
according to a specific pattern.
Can you fill in the blank section?

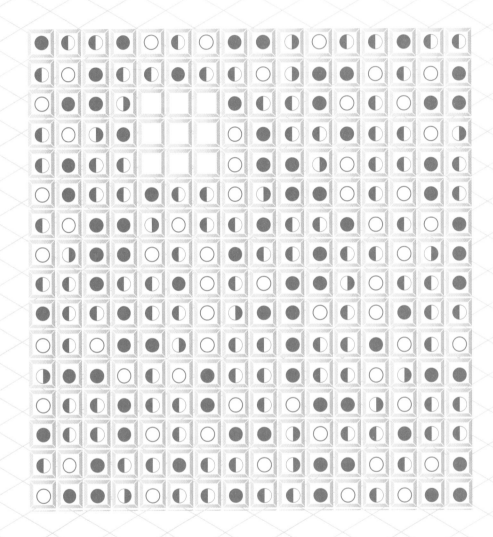

Answer see page 144

THE
ANSWERS

01

B. (Initial letter of the location is the fourth letter of the name.)

02

63 (= 17+12+17+17).

03

022, 185, 348, 511, 674, 837

04

Cardiff (The others are in England.)

05

Bee Gees, Saturday Night Fever. Whitney Houston, The Bodyguard. Pink Floyd, The Dark Side of the Moon. Celine Dion, Falling Into You.

06

1 honest and 99 corrupt.

07

a6

08

6	8	3	5	2
8	0	1	5	1
3	1	7	6	9
5	5	6	4	8
2	1	9	8	2

09

Bottom centre. (The small cross should be diagonal, not orthogonal.)

10

11

Uganda, Australia, Czech Republic, Mexico, Scotland.

12

10. (2+2+3+3)

13

21*31 = 651

14

European capitals alternate with random cities, but Frankfurt is not the capital of Germany; it should be Berlin.

15

Potassium. Manganese. Molybdenum. Phosphorus. Hydrogen.

16

Copenhagen, Georgetown, Bratislava

17

The 2L tile that's in row 2 and column 3, where 1,1 is the top left corner.

18

W (sequence skips 2 letters, then 1, then 0).

19

Weapons: flamberge, guisarme, chakram.
Languages: Ablaite, Palaic, Ugaritic.
Colours: Amaranthine, celadon, sanguineous.
Fish: barbel, snook, rasbora.

20

2. The 'true' sequence is the top row + first digit of second row: 1 5 3 7 2 6 4 8 0 9.

21

12 (L=13, M=17, N=11).

22

1. (Number of rectangles enclosing value)

23

T (Triangulated).

24

Manhattan, Bronx, Brooklyn, Queens, Staten Island.

25

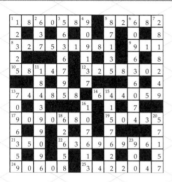

26

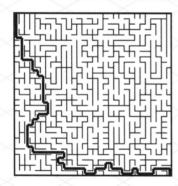

27

O.

28

PE. (Puli, Tosa, Skye, Chow)

29

4. (H=8, D=4, 8-4=4)

30

R. (cigar, brink, crows, smart).

31

Z. (Outer = Middle + Centre).

32

Marrakesh.

33

6 days. (In six days, both moons will be at 72 degrees to their starting point, making a straight line.)

34

27	21	22	18	33
19	29	28	22	23
23	24	20	30	24
31	25	19	25	21
21	22	32	26	20

35

B. (The others were all battles of the American Civil War).

36

G.

37

5 (Total=35).

38

D. (It has the two boxes overlapping by one corner each, with the circle overlapping an adjacent corner.)

39

D. (Whizzbangs)

40

A orange square.

41

42

D. (It is the only one containing shapes with no straight lines.)

43

1154 (*6, *17, *235, *12, *3, *21).

44

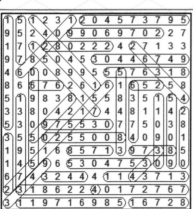

45

H. (The gap between letters increases by one each time.)

46

45.

47

F.

48

D.

49

3059056 and **3719534**.

50

Fortification.

51

6.

52

Pings Hip (= shipping. Others are **dinheiro** (Portugal), **drachma** (Greece), **guilder**, (British Guiana), **koruna** (Czech Republic), **ostmark** (East Germany).

53

54

7.

55

E.

56

Powers of 5 (5^9 to 5^18).

57

761 (*47, *4, *476, *19, *9, *158).

58

6 (each segment totals 21)

59

792.

60

42 (=9+9+9+7+8)

61

H.

62

The figure would have two hands and two feet

63

P (All letters represent the number of their position in the alphabet. Intersection is sum of top circle, difference between letters of bottom circle).

64

A.

65

13. (Each number is equal to the sum of the two before it, starting with (0,1) as the initial pair. This is the Fibonacci sequence.)

66

67

4 (y=2, a=1, b=3, c=5).

68

10128233 (= 6703*1511), **27140447** (= 6703*4049), **52839749** (= 6703*7883).

69

2 * 16lbs and 4 * 17lbs.

70

Triangular Numbers

71

Yellow triangle. (The centre symbol equal to one of the outer circles – in the first diagram, it is the bottom left symbol, and in each subsequent diagram, it advances one place clockwise round the circle.)

72

137

```
H S Ⓢ P S I S H H S I I A S S
S S D D H I I A D P A A D S D
A I I A P D H S D A I A A P I
I A H P H A I A A A P D P P D
P D P H H I H D S D D H D I A
A P Ⓐ S P I S I D P P D D A I
I P A I D I I A H I A I S I I
P I I I I A P D P I S H H P S
H A A P D A H I A A A P I H P
H D A S I I D D A I A P S P A
S A S S D A A S I S S S I H H
D A I P P S H I I S H S D S P
S D S D A I D I P D A S I D S
I A S A I I A A S I A I H P D
I P A S D P I D S S S P D I H
```

73

33. (Taking the letters as being worth a number equal to their position in the alphabet, increase the size of the gap to the next number by one each time.)

74

Dubai, Tomsk, Perth, Essen, Kyoto

75

0. (Second row subtracts from first row to give third row.)

76

8 (= 6 * 4 / 3)

77

19 (Add the two outer, horizontally adjacent numbers together, subtract the remaining outer number, and put the result in the inner cell of the diagonally opposite square).

78

152843769, 412739856, 653927184, 735982641, 326597184.

79

8 + 4 − 3 x 2 − 7 + 5 − 9 = 7

80

6 (E = The last digit of A+B)

81

 (After each repetition, the first two symbols are dropped)

82

35. (The others are prime)

83

Y. The first circle contains letters with horizontal symmetry.

84

4. (743-489=254)

85

Prime numbers.

86

11:25. (The hour hand goes back by two hours each time, and the minute hand forward by 25 minutes.)

87

A (rectangle)

88

B (The letters represent numbers based on their position in the alphabet, and in each row, the first column minus the second column equals the third column.)

89

1827049536.

90

91

B. (Treating the letters as the numerical value of their position in the alphabet, in each column, the top row − the middle row = the bottom row.)

92

3 (in C, numbers from B are alternately doubled or halved).

93

Our answer is (23 + 8 − 1) / 10 * 5 = (8 * 2) - 1.

94

i, n.

95

25. (Each number pairs with another to sum to 50.)

96

D. (Reading across, the second letter is as far past the first letter into the alphabet as the first was in from the start. So E > J, G > N, and B > D.)

97

One solution is 1024 *7 = 7168 / 4 = 1792 * 3 = 5376 / 2 = 2688.

98

30.

99

(next segment=) 576, (first prime<576=) 571, ((576-571)*5=) 25.

100

A5. The grid represents the numbers 1-100, and the dots are the prime numbers.

101

Fibonacci numbers (24th to 33rd in the sequence).

102

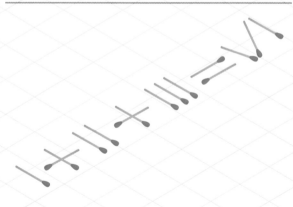

103

The 6D tile that's in row 1 and column 6, where 1,1 is the top left corner.

104

M. (Each circle is an 8-letter word backwards)

105

N. (The dominos contain the initial letters of the elements on the periodic table.)

106

Vera Cruz

107

22	33	16	35	9
34	9	21	31	20
30	18	38	8	21
12	20	30	17	36
17	35	10	24	29

108

5 (9-4=).

109

Square numbers.

110

3187 (*17, *54, *2, *26, *85, *23)

111

-14. (-2 + -5 + -2 + -5).

112

Flip twice. If you get either two heads or two tails, flip again. If you have one of each, assign H-T to one option, and T-H to the other. However biased it is, it will always have the same chance of generating T-H as H-T.

113

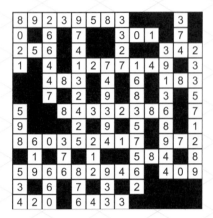

114

13. The 'true' sequence is: 638012503140.

115

10 and ²/₇ths days. (In 10 and ²/₇ths days, the faster moon will be at 51 and ³/₇ths degrees to its origin, having completed one circuit and started its second, whilst the slower moon will be precisely opposite the planet from it, at 231 and ³/₇ths degrees to its origin.)

116

Anna Karenina, Leo Tolstoy.

117

W ((2*18) + 2 – 15 = 23). Letters represent numbers in alphabetic position.

118

627953481, 847159236, 923187456, 215384976, 537219684.

119

A Yellow square with a small blue square in the top right. (The 8-block pattern runs clockwise around the larger squares from top left, inverting tone and rotating one place anticlockwise after completion).

120

2. 'W' = 1, 'X' = 2, 'Y' = 4, 'Z' = 4

121

1	●		●	2		●	4	●		●	
		3	3	3	●	3	3	●	●	4	2	2
●		●			●	2			●		
●	●	3	3		2		1				
2			●	●				●		2	●
0			2	2		0	2	●	●		2
			1	1				2	3		●
1	●		●			0	0		●	●
2	3			1				3	
●	3	●	●	2		1	1	3	●	2
●			3	3	●		●	4	●	2
●	2	0		●	2	1		●	2

122

1 (9761271 =*18664, 3913086=*7482, 1868679=*3573, 2504124 =*4788, 8013929 =*15323).

123

Our answer is ((13 + 5) * 6 + 4) / 16 = (6^2 – 8) / 4.

124

5 (2+3; the 7 is unused.)

125

12.6.

126

4975883 and **7505993** (*59 and *89).

127

B. (It is formed of five identically-shaped polygons of differing sizes which overlap each other but do not contain each other.)

128

C.

129

Giuseppe Arcimboldo, The Fire. Max Beckmann, Actors Triptych. Frits Van den Berghe, Sunday. Francisco Goya, Carnival Scene. Vincent van Gogh, Self-portrait

130

6. (Consider the second row as a single number, double it, and add it to the first row, also as a single number, to get the value of the entire third row.)

131

3:29 and 40 seconds. (The hour and minute increase each time by a regularly increasing amount, 1h 22m the first time, 2h 33m the second, and so on. The second hand increases by ten seconds.)

132

1298.

133

134

Regoliths

135

Anaconda, Ibis, Echidna, Quetzal, Anteater.

136

D (Six-pointed star).

137

5 (DE = AB - C, treating AB and DE as two-digit numbers).

138

◐ (When the pattern comes to the end of its cycle, it reverses direction.)

139

D. (The others were all prime minsters of the United Kingdom.)

140

20. (Each number groups with two others in forming the 3rd, 5th, and 8th multiple of a base number. 5*4 is missing.).

141

The RATS numbers, "Reverse Add, Then Sort", where to find each new term, you add the previous term to the number obtained by reversing the digits of that same previous term, and then you put the digits of the answer in ascending order – so 16+61 is 77. (5th to 17th in the sequence).

142

It contains all ten digits once, in English alphabetical order.

143

D.

144

V. (devas, breve, valet, ovine).

145

L. (Treating the letters as the numerical value of their position in the alphabet, in each column, the top row of the previous column + the middle row of the previous column = the bottom row.)

146

N, which should be 'M'. Each letter in the second circle is 8 places further along the alphabet than a letter in the first circle.

147

B.

148

8	4	2	7	6
4	3	1	1	9
2	1	2	5	0
7	1	5	9	1
6	9	0	1	8

149

H6. (The grid represents the numbers 100 down to 1, and the dots are the squares.)

150

106, 255, 404, 553, 702, 851

151

0 (L=5, M=-13, N=42).

152

E. (Initial letter of the team is the final letter of the next person's name when arranged in a clockwise circle)

153

29 (= 10+4+7+8).

154

9 * 7 – 18 / 5 + 23 * 2 / 8 = 8

155

4 (all three circles total to 80).

156

Centre left. (The unbroken mid-size circle is missing.)

157

I.

158

90-31=59

159

5 of each. (5*6)+(5*5)=(56-1)

160

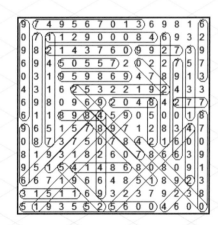

161

D. (It is the only one to have a box whose sides intersect no other sides.)

162

Mount McKinley, Kilimanjaro, Pico de Orizaba, Popocatepetl, Ben Macdhui.

163

One solution is 1344* 7 = 9408 / 3 = 3136 / 8 = 392 * 5 = 1960.

164

37. (The term increases, each time, by the odd numbers in increasing order, starting with 1.)

165

9814072356

166

R (13+9-4 = 24-2-4=18).

167

D. (The others are individual islands)

168

e, l, n

169

55. (The others form pairs in which each number is the other with the order of the digits reversed.)

170

38 (=7+8+8+9+6).

171

5 (The rings hold the prime numbers in order, from the centre of the upper left segment to the outer, then from the outer back to the inner of the second segment, and so on.)

172

The figure would be missing the right leg.

173

f3

174

Squares = 121, 144, 441; Primes = 101, 211, 421; Happy = 44, 100, 440; Divisors of 888 = 111, 222, 444

175

2. (Number of sides immediately surrounding value).

176

Superior, Michigan, Huron, Erie, Ontario.

177

9 (679 – 385 = 294).

178

FN. (Converting letters into numbers, the outer circle is the middle circle to the power of the inner circle. The values of the outer circle are given as a form of base 26 that uses the letters A-Z as digits.)

179

9. (Clockwise from left, and replacing numbers with the letter in that position of the alphabet, the entries in the grid spell out RATIONALISTS.)

180

Yellow circle. (Add the number of sides of the symbols around the centre to find how many sides the central symbol should have. Solid symbols are positive, outline symbols are negative.)

181

5 (6228-2408 = 3675 = 7495 -3675).

182

40.

183

Chambertin, a wine. (The cheeses are roquefort, lymsewold, camembert, wensleydale, and red leicester.)

184

27 (4096, 6400, 7921, 8836).

185

5.

186

187

Largest prime number of X digits (X = 4 to 13).

188

6 (y=1, a=7, b=3, c=4).

189

```
O S N S I O M S S I O N I U I
L U S U M U N U S U L U U O N
M U N O I S N U M L U S L N S
S O I S U O O L U N S L S O I
I U U L M U L U M I U L S U N
L M S U M N M N U S I S M I O
S N U I N I I S I M L O M U S
I M I U I U L O U L I L M O N
I N O O (S U O N I M U L) S N N
M U O N U L O O U U U O L M U
O N U S I U L O M S M S N I L
L U M U U I S M L I U N M O L
L O U M M I S I U N U S S S I
I L N O O I O L O O S L N M O
N N L L I L S O O M S U U O I
```

190

491. (Working inwards, n – (n+1) = (n+2)
Absolute).

191

A towel.

192

L. All the others possess at least one degree
of symmetry.

193

5 (Add the outer 3 numbers together, then add
the digits of that result together to find the inner
number)

194

353 (*95, *887, *209, *83, *11).

195

Montevideo, Libreville, Willemstad

196

Congo, Indus, Yukon, Tiber, Rhone

197

665. (7!/2!5! * 5!/3!2! + 7!/3!4! * 5!/2!3! + 7!/4!3! *
5!/1!4!).

198

D. (The dominos spell out the word KNOTWEED.)

199

The Ionian is a sea. All the others are bays.

200

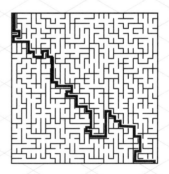

201

491. Pattern runs right then back left, from top left.